DR. LANCE WALLNAU

GOD'S CHAOS CANDIDATE

DONALD J. TRUMP AND THE AMERICAN UNRAVELING

KILLER SHEEP MEDIA, INC.

GOD'S CHAOS CANDIDATE
DONALD J. TRUMP AND THE AMERICAN UNRAVELING

Printed in the USA

Published by Killer Sheep Media, Inc., Keller, TX 76248

Cover Design by Chelsea Hicks and Mercedes Sparks
Author Photo by Michaella McClendon
Edited by an anonymous "Ninja Sheep" warrior along with Elizabeth Prestwood

ISBN (Print): 978-0-9982164-0-9

ISBN (Kindle): 978-0-9982164-1-6

www.lancewallnau.com
www.godschaoscandidate.com

KILLER SHEEP MEDIA, INC.

DEDICATION

Dedicated to Annabelle Wallnau, the secret sauce behind me and everything our organization does. Thank you, Annabelle—my love, my best friend, and my wife of 30 years.

I can't wait to read your book ...

ACKNOWLEDGEMENT

I wish to make a special acknowledgment to Kim Clement, the amazing prophetic voice who helped me find my own.

The invitation to meet with Donald Trump at Trump Towers was set for September 14, 2015. I thought it interesting that this date coincided with a "Blood Moon" (9/13), as well as the Jewish Feast of Trumpets. I was looking forward to seeing my friend, Kim Clement, at this meeting. A few years earlier Kim prophesied that Trump would be "God's Trumpet," so I was especially interested in Kim's perception of Trump and his future. However, just before the meeting with Trump, Kim suffered a stroke and was engaged in the fight of his life. I never got to hear Kim's updated thoughts about Mr. Trump. Without Kim's perception to add to mine, I took my time and researched Trump and the prophetic trajectory of America for a whole year following this initial meeting in New York.

Now the finished product is in your hands. The book on Trump started during the Feast of Trumpets 2015 and went to print a year later, by divine coincidence, during the Feast of Trumpets 2016. May Kim's initial word on Trump being God's Trumpet be fulfilled exactly as God desired.

CONTENTS

CHAPTER 1—   7

AMERICA'S FOURTH CRUCIBLE

CHAPTER 2—   35

THE CAMPAIGN BEGINS

CHAPTER 3—   45

THE BOARDROOM

CHAPTER 4—   55

"I'M NOT MICHAEL COHEN!"

CHAPTER 5—   63

THEN I HEARD THE WORDS, "COMMON GRACE!"

CHAPTER 6—   73

THE GOSPEL IN BLACK AND WHITE

CHAPTER 7—   83

THE CONVENTION

CHAPTER 8—   97

"LEAD US NOT INTO TRUMPTATION ..."

CHAPTER 9—   121

THE GREAT AMERICAN UNRAVELING

CHAPTER 10—   137

THE UNFINISHED ASSIGNMENT

APPENDIX—   151

SNAPSHOT OF THE 2016 REPUBLICAN PARTY PLATFORM

CHAPTER 1

AMERICA'S
FOURTH CRUCIBLE

Make no mistake, that gnawing concern you have about the future of our nation is not delusional. While it's trendy in Christian circles to make fun of those who see trouble ahead, the Bible makes it clear: *"By faith Noah, being warned by God concerning events as yet unseen, in reverent fear constructed an ark for the saving of his household"* (Hebrews 11:7).

Noah wasn't paranoid—he was perceptive.

When Jeb Bush referred to Donald Trump as "the chaos candidate,"[1] he may have been tapping into something more prophetic than he was aware. America is already in chaos and heading into what I am referring to as the Fourth American Crucible.

I remember when the Lord spoke to me about Donald Trump, at a time when there were still 15 or so candidates contending for the nomination. I heard in my spirit: *Donald Trump is a wrecking ball to the spirit of political correctness.* I wondered how this wrecking ball would be used. What I heard—and will share with you in this book—will surprise you.

Most people forget what was happening when Trump first emerged.

You could hear the eggshells under the soft feet of Christians trying to respond thoughtfully to "safe spaces" on campuses, Caitlyn Jenner on the cover of *Vanity Fair,* illegal immigration on the border and riots in Ferguson and Baltimore. The Supreme Court made same sex marriage legal and the President celebrated the decision by lighting up the White House in rainbow colors. Incidents of homegrown terror, border invasion and crime were ignored by leaders in both parties as talks continued about increasing refugee immigration from Syria. The Islamic State of Iraq and Syria (ISIS) was on a rampage—specifically targeting Christians—but no one wanted to talk about this aspect of ISIS. In the midst of these controversies the church in America seemed confused, anxious and strangely quiet.

If the church seemed silent, it wasn't idle. Leaders were actively looking for the hopeful deliverer—a conservative Christian presidential candidate who would make things right.

Into this setting, a rugged wilderness voice emerged—Donald J. Trump. The moment he began speaking the entire conversation shifted. Trump gave nervous evangelicals a gift that many of them lacked—the gift of boldness. Here was a man who had opinions. He didn't speak in the calculated talking points of a politician. His delivery, with a slight accent from Queens, NY, was simple and direct. His emergence is such a destabilizing threat to the vast deal making machinery embedded in both parties that he has the unique distinction of being rejected by both liberal Democrats and establishment Republicans at the same time.

Who or What Is Really Behin This—the Shadow Cabinet:

I don't think that Trump himself understands the full extent of the apparatus this wrecking ball is hitting. Most Christians don't know the nature and extent of the organization they are up against. They just know that the deterioration of America has accelerated over the last decade. They never uncovered the machinery that was built to break down and destroy the influence of conservatives and Christians. In fact, this shadow cabinet[2] is the best kept secret of the Progressive Left. After the election losses in 2000, the Left realized that it needed to rebuild its movement. A handful of smart and extremely wealthy liberals decided it was time to close the gap on the Republicans' enormous advantage in grassroots organizing and evangelical influence. The strategists came together and called themselves the "Thunder Road Group,"[3] based on the opening track of Bruce Springsteen's 1975 breakthrough album *Born to Run*. When they were finished, things would definitely be run differently in America.

Much like Nehemiah walking around the walls of Jerusalem, they did a 360 degree assessment of the strengths of the conservative movement. Where they saw strength they created a counter strategy to call into existence new single issue organizations that would target each of these areas and break them down. In essence, they laid siege works against the conservative movement's greatest strengths. Where no Leftist organization existed to take on the task, they created one. When campaign finance was reformed a loophole was found. This loophole allowed for the creation of organizations called 527's—associations organized for the purpose of influencing an issue and capable of receiving unlimited funds! Think of Thunder Road as a gathering of apostolic progressives determined to disciple America according to their vision and you'll see why I am worked up about this—and you should be too!

- They needed a think tank, so they created Center for American Progress.

- They needed a media operation for all the 527s, so they created The Media Fund and Media Matters.

- They needed to dig up dirt in opposition research, so they created Citizens for Responsibility and Ethics in Washington (CREW).

- They needed to organize Hollywood and hold concerts to get out the vote, so they created America Votes.

- They needed a vast funding source, so with George Soros' help they created Open Society and Democracy Alliance.[4]

- They needed a social technology movement, so they drafted MoveOn.Org.

Once their strategy was in place, they called together a private audience with 100 leaders who could each contribute 1 million dollars to the new strategy. With 100 million dollars they began to remake America!

Over the years this group has grown and become the most powerful political coalition in history—built and sustained by coordinated giving and a central strategy.

Thunder Road built a siege engine, a machine whose infrastructure now dwarfs conservatism's in size, scope and sophistication. It has been setting and helping to impose the national agenda that has changed

America since 2000, and it kicked into high gear with President Obama in 2008. Since then it has morphed and expanded like Professor Moriarty's underground web.

Which brings us back to the "chaos candidate." No one in American history has been better poised to set back the progress of progressives and tear through the web than the wrecking ball himself.

While Men Slept

But are most evangelicals even awake to what's happening in this hour? The Parable of Jesus regarding the end-time harvest could not be more relevant to our times: "*But while everyone was sleeping, his enemy came and sowed weeds among the wheat, and went away*" (Matthew 13:25). Note the state of the people Jesus described. They were asleep, unconscious and unaware of what was going on. The disciples, wanting further clarity on what Jesus meant, asked him to explain.

"*The field is the world, and the good seed stands for the people of the kingdom. The weeds are the people of the evil one.*" The meaning could not be more obvious—in the very place where God wants a harvest, Satan plants people who attempt to disrupt the harvest!

America is unraveling at the seams because a powerful group of Americans—the "shadow cabinet"—want it to. They are a group of billionaires and millionaires, politicians, consultants, academics and activists. This is not a very large group. It is a small number of people exerting a great deal of influence. This can't be emphasized enough. This is a minority of people who are succeeding in bullying the majority of the people in this country. This little group does not represent all liberals, but their access to media and academia intimidates those who would like to push back against them.[5]

11

But know this: The decline you see is not an accident—it is a policy objective. Since the 1960's, there has been a continuous movement at work to remake America. And now we have come to the defining moment. If this decline continues for one more presidential cycle, America as we know it will cease to exist.

The church has a "Great Commission" to disciple nations that takes us into seven spheres. We call this the 7 Mountain Strategy. Curiously, Thunder Road executes its strategy through these same seven spheres of influence. These seven institutions, or mountains, are the gates of influence that progressives seek to penetrate and dominate. Once occupied, these domains are shaped by their ideas. In essence, these seven institutions are being transformed into the image and likeness of those who dominate them. The seven institutions are the prime real-estate that shapes culture. If you wonder where the "gates of hell" are located, you should look no further than the summits of these mountains. Proximity is power. There will always be a battle for who is at the top of these seven mountains. Those gatekeepers shape the nations. The devil himself takes an interest in who rules kingdoms. When the devil showed Jesus all the kingdoms of this world he boasted, *All this has been given to me and I give it to whom I will.* There is a lot of selfish ambition, deception and corrupt deal making at the top of the seven mountains. Temptation is always greatest where money, power and influence overlap. But this is also the place where influence is greatest.

Let us take a look at the seven mountains of culture that make up our nation:

1. Religion

2. Family

3. Education

4. Government

5. News Media

6. Entertainment

7. Business/Economics.

If you are a Christian, you can go down the list and mark the progress of Progressives from redefining marriage to targeting Christian bakers, florists, photographers and wedding chapels to put them out of business. In education, progressives use new textbooks like Howard Zinn's alternate interpretation of the history of the United States—an interpretation of history that shames and blames America. These false teachers use false doctrine to disciple the next generation of America-hating leaders. They want a revolution and they are so close they can taste it.

Believers who obsess over President Obama's role in the unraveling of America miss the big picture. He is not the architect—he is the accelerator. Thunder Road is the "shadow cabinet" behind the scenes coordinating the uprisings and media coverage, but there is a spirit even behind that. The root can be defined as a powerful resurgence of a lawless spirit that is rooted in the radicals of the 1960s. The difference between 1960 and now is that the radicals have changed their tactics and learned how to achieve their desired end result. The protesters became the professors and

> BELIEVERS WHO OBSESS OVER OBAMA'S ROLE IN THE UNRAVELING OF AMERICA MISS THE BIG PICTURE

the disciples of Saul Alinsky have become the apostles of community organizing at a national level. They do so by taking seats at the gates of influence where they have the power to shape and manipulate public policy and perception.

Author Dinesh D'Souza says, "What makes the plan especially chilling is that most Americans are simply unaware of what's going on. Their ignorance, as we shall see, is part of the plan. It should be emphasized at the outset that the domestic champions of American decline are not traitors or America-haters. They are bringing down America because they genuinely believe that America deserves to be brought down. Their actions are the result of a powerful moral critique of America, one that has never been effectively answered."[6]

America Unraveling

Compared to other nations, America is relatively young. Yet America has already experienced three significant times of testing—crucibles—that have defined us as a nation. Understanding the three American crucibles is of massive importance, and it is my belief that we are now facing the fourth.

- **The first crucible** involved the founding of our nation and we know it as the American Revolution, 1775-1783.

- **The second crucible** was the Civil War, 1860-1865. Abraham Lincoln writes of civil war as a *"testing whether that nation, or any nation so conceived and so dedicated, can long endure."*[7]

- **The third crucible** was the Great Depression, 1929-1939, and World War II, 1939-1945. It was a test of our survival as a nation.

- **The fourth crucible is upon us**.

We are already witnessing the first phase of the "unraveling"— race wars, class wars, and religious wars as Islamic terror incidents at home add to the combustion. All of this is the intentional destabilizing prelude to the great economic "reset."

The trigger for this fourth crucible could come from any number of global incidents, but whatever the cause, it will most likely manifest in regional social upheavals and a national economic meltdown. It can be swift or prolonged. It can be very severe or less severe. Much depends on the governing philosophy that enters the White House in 2016. This factor more than any other will shape America and the world for better or worse.

Just How Close Are We?

The first wave of "crisis" has already begun to manifest. The period we are in could be called "The Great Unraveling" as the nation shakes, but the real catalyst to revolution in America is not religious, racial or a matter of sexual orientation—it is economic!

Under President Obama we have gone from $10 trillion to $19 trillion in debt. The fiscal breaking point is $20-$21 trillion—we are that close! We are propping up America by printing Monopoly money (called quantitative easing) and setting ourselves up to become a banana republic with triple digit runaway inflation like Venezuela or Zimbabwe. Wall Street is a bubble right now, much like the housing market of 2008. The only difference is that we can't bail ourselves out again.

Before WWII, Britain dominated world trade. After the war, global trade shifted toward the United States, putting the U.S. dollar at the forefront of international finance. But now China has surpassed

America as the largest merchandise trader in the world. The pattern is clear. When a country dominates world trade, it becomes the world's primary currency. For years I've heard prophets say that China will overtake the United States as the world economic power by 2016-2017. I'm shocked by the enthusiasm of believers who hear these things. Do you think China is Gospel friendly? Really? If history is any indicator, the Yuan will be the next primary currency. As we speak, China is seeking to be a reserve currency. What happens to America if China is successful? It's fairly possible that we'll see the U.S. dollar collapse. If that happens and inflation spirals, our money will be as worthless as confederate dollar bills were after the civil war.

How Bad Can It Get?

You can already see what's happening to America. Radical progressives are trying to ride the wave of social unrest in order to trigger a socialist reset of America. It is up to you and me to resist this remaking of America.

It will be hard to stop, however, if we wait till "America goes on sale," and foreign nations settle up with our debt by buying our assets, major corporations, real estate and even national parks. In the future, Americans out of work may reach levels not seen since the Great Depression. Families will have to share apartments and living spaces as home ownership will be a luxury. The number of homeless people will surge.

Heidi Baker, a respected global missionary, shared a vision she received while visiting a church in the United States. She was almost hesitant to share it because the host church had a strong emphasis on faith and victory: "I saw bread lines, soup kitchens, and I saw people wearing beautiful clothing. Their clothing was not worn out … I didn't want to see what I saw, but I saw what I saw … I was so undone, that I just said what I saw. And I saw all these people and they had beautiful cars, 4 x 4s and Lexus, Mercedes, BMWs, Toyotas, there they were with fancy shiny cars, but they were standing in line." The word she heard was "suddenly." She also saw "worriers" become "warriors" and miracles similar to what she has seen in Mozambique.

Let's dismiss the economics of an unraveling and assume that it does not happen. How else will America be forever changed after the presidential election of 2016?

Hugh Hewitt makes this observation:

> If Hillary Clinton wins, the Left gavels in a solid, lasting, almost certainly permanent majority on the Supreme Court. Every political issue has a theoretical path to SCOTUS, and only self-imposed judicial restraint has checked the Supreme Court's appetite and reach for two centuries.

> That restraint will be gone when Hillary Rodham Clinton's first appointee is sworn in. Finished. This is not hyperbole. I have the advantage of having taught Conservative Law for 20 years, of having argued before very liberal appellate judges like Judge Stephen Reinhardt of the very liberal Ninth Circuit, of practicing with the best litigators in the land. I know what a very liberal Supreme Court means: Conservatism is done. It cannot survive a strong-willed liberal majority on the

Supreme Court. Every issue—EVERY issue—will end up there, and the legislature's judgments will matter not a bit.[8]

Imagine the impact on religious liberty and free speech when courts with a liberal majority hear cases by the "Human Rights Campaign"—America's largest civil rights organization advancing lesbian, gay, bisexual and transgender equality.

The Next Generation of Leaders

When Christians read about "doctrines of demons," "false Christs," and "false teachers," who or what do you think Scripture is talking about? The territory to watch isn't always in the church—it's a call to keep an eye on our government, universities and thought leaders. Watch who is shaping the minds of the populace and what they are feeding them!

What if the "false doctrine" today isn't so much the teaching of nutty preachers on the radio as it is the teaching of nutty professors in schools and universities? What if the "false prophets" and "counterfeit apostles" we should look for are not emerging from religious cults, but rather progressive politics? Look at the myriad of well-funded, single-issue activist organizations on the Left. What if we saw this as a counterfeit evangelism movement? What do evangelists do? They go out and make converts. You think I am joking? This is what we are up against. In many ways they are showing us what we must do. Why do you think we lost so much ground for the last decade in spite of revival ministries and church growth flourishing? Jesus taught that "tares" are people the devil plants, and he plants them to entangle and thwart the harvest of God. This is the story of the United States. While we preached and prayed, the Left discipled the nation.

Perhaps we need our own Thunder Road?

The Role of Prophetic Leaders in Crisis

Winston Churchill was mocked by his contemporaries because of his constant tirades about "Herr Hitler" and the threat he was becoming to all of Europe. The public simply did not want to see the reality of the threat that was facing them. Instead, they wanted what Neville Chamberlain gave them—a useless piece of paper—a promise of "peace in our time." The problem was that England wanted peace in a time of war.

Churchill ended up the true prophet who saw the threat for what it was. He explained the cost of not taking action, and when the time came to lead he laid out the price of victory in blood, sweat and tears.

Churchill was a prophetic leader.

He was—as I will explain in a moment—God's "Cyrus." He was raised up during WWII as the instrument to stop Hitler. Churchill saw the bigger issues and described the grand theme of their crisis as a contest involving the survival of "Christian civilization."

I have Churchill's memoirs in my library and I think you'll find the titles of the first three books quite prophetic for our day:

1. *The Gathering Storm*

2. *Their Finest Hour*

3. *The Grand Alliance*

The Gathering Storm tells of Churchill's critical observations on the settlement of WWI and its role in the causes of WWII, which reminds me of what many of us feel now—that gnawing concern for our nation's future.

Their Finest Hour is the story of the remnant of Royal Air Force pilots who stopped the German invasion—in the air! It reminds me how a properly mobilized remnant can make a difference against great odds. The battle is fought "up there," so to speak, in the spirit realm.

The Grand Alliance describes how the Allied Nations finally started working together collaboratively "as one" to defeat their common enemy.

Trump's Churchillian Perspective

I see many similarities between Donald Trump and Winston Churchill—especially in the ways Churchill grated on the nerves of his contemporaries by saying things they didn't want to hear and describing things others didn't want to see. Churchill had an ability to prophetically intuit what was coming. He saw the world in a particular way and would not back down.

After Donald Trump finished his nomination speech at the Republican National Convention in Cleveland, Ohio on July 21, 2016, his critics described his speech as "dark" and "dystopian." They were turned off by his "relentlessly grim" and "gloomy" picture of America. What really happened? Trump gave a Churchillian assessment of America on its current course. In contrast, the Democratic National

Convention was an upbeat beating-down of Trump. It was like watching a celebrity dance party on the deck of the Titanic.

The liberal media's response was 100 percent in agreement that Trump's speech would cost him votes. They were shocked when they discovered that 75 percent of the viewers said his speech had a "very positive" or "somewhat positive" effect.[9] The media may have been shocked, but I wasn't. I was not taken by surprise because 73 percent of Americans believe the country is on the wrong track.[10]

To a great extent this explains something about Trump's supporters and his critics. President Barack Obama intentionally ran as a blank slate upon which you could write anything. You could give him whatever qualities you were looking for. Trump is the opposite. He is a mirror that reflects back the worldview of the beholder. If you have a lawless spirit, Trump is your bad cop. If you are an open borders, open arms type of person, Trump is the Grinch that stole Christmas. If you are concerned about the future of America, he is a potential answer to prayer.

Donald Trump: The Wrecking Ball

As I said earlier, prior to my first meeting with Trump I heard the Lord say to me, "Donald Trump is a wrecking ball to the spirit of political correctness!"

I published this prophetic word right away, exactly as I heard it, at the beginning of the 2016 Primary Election season. I did not know exactly what this meant, other than the fact that he would be used to challenge and disrupt the nation's political discourse. That first meeting was wild. Virtually everything I needed to know about

Trump was there. (I will tell you about this landmark meeting in a later chapter.)

Cyrus the 45th Chapter

It was prior to my second meeting with Trump that I ran across an unusual image on my computer. It was a picture of Trump seated in the Oval Office with these words: **"Donald Trump 45th President of the United States."** The image made a peculiar impression on me. With literally 17 candidates running to be the Republican presidential nominee, no one, including me, was thinking of Donald Trump as president. I wanted to return to my work but could not shake the image. It struck me the same way the "wrecking ball" word did.

I was curious about whether or not the next president would be America's 45th president. *That can't be right*, I thought, *Is Barack Obama the 44th president?* Sure enough, he is the 44th president, and when he was re-elected for his second term, the number stayed 44. In 2016, we will elect the 45th president of the United States.

Immediately after that, I heard the Lord say, "Read Isaiah 45."

Now I don't pretend to hear God all the time, so the few times I do hear it stands out. I had a King James Version Bible near me and began to read: *"Thus says the LORD to **his anointed, to Cyrus**, whose right hand I have grasped, to subdue nations before him and to loose the belts of kings, to open doors before him that gates may not be closed"* (Isaiah 45:1).

Cyrus, I thought? *Who is he again? How does this matter to America right now?*

Here's what I found: In Isaiah 45, God prophesied that He would raise up a ruler named Cyrus, and this was announced 150 years before the man was born. Cyrus is mentioned by name 30 times in the Bible, and it was the Cyrus decree that authorized the return of the Jews to Jerusalem to rebuild the house of God. It was also this decree that empowered Nehemiah to build his wall.

Isaiah predicted that Cyrus would virtually walk right into Babylon and take it, and in 539 B.C. a man named Cyrus did just that—he took Babylon without a struggle. According to the Greek historian Herodotus, his army diverted the course of the Euphrates River, making the river level drop and giving the invading forces the ability to enter into the city that night through the riverbed. It was just as Isaiah the prophet said, prophesying to Babylon, *"I will dry up your rivers"* (Isaiah 44:27).

The Bible tells us that as the Babylonian King Belteshazzar and his friends were drunk with wine, no one had noticed that the waters in the Euphrates were diminishing. Cyrus marched his armies across the riverbed. Just as Isaiah wrote, the gates would *"not be closed"* (Isaiah 45:1), and the Persians easily entered the city through the open gates. *'That very night Belteshazzar, king of the Babylonians, was slain"* (Daniel 5:30).

Within a year, Cyrus declared all the Jews held captive in Babylon were to be set free and allowed to return home to Jerusalem, as described in Ezra 1. These two events—the taking of Babylon the Great, without a battle, and the freeing of the Jews soon after—are both remarkable historical events tied to a prophecy in Isaiah 150 years before they occurred. I find it remarkable that God calls people to specific tasks before they were born, don't you?

The Cyrus Cylinder

Centuries later, Hormonz Rassam, while exploring an excavated site in Babylon in 1879, made one of history's greatest archaeological discoveries. He held in his hand the fragile "Cyrus Cylinder"!

The Cyrus Cylinder is an artifact, dating back to the time of Daniel, between 538-529 B.C., that records the destruction of the Babylonian empire and the return of the Jewish people to Palestine from their captivity. This confirms what the Bible tells us, and here's what I find interesting about that: according to the cylinder, this ruler dealt with three issues we have today—terrorism, faith and the economic well-being of the people.

Here's the part dictated by Cyrus himself: *"I did not allow any to terrorize the land of Sumer and Akkad. I kept in view the needs of Babylon and all its sanctuaries to promote their well-being. The citizens of Babylon. I lifted their unbecoming yoke. Their dilapidated dwellings I restored. I put an end to their misfortunes."*

Why should this discovery matter to us? Because the idea of God raising up "Isaiah 45" secular leaders who are anointed to help God's people build healthy nations is a GAME CHANGER for us! Cyrus was an anointed, secular ruler raised up through the intercession of God's people. Isaiah calls Cyrus, "My anointed," yet this man was not a Jew. He was a king outside the royal lineage of Hebrew kings.

> THE IDEA OF GOD RAISING UP SECULAR LEADERS WHO ARE ANOINTED TO BUILD HEALTHY NATIONS IS A GAME CHANGER

As Daniel's time in office overlapped with Cyrus, it is entirely conceivable that he influenced Cyrus regarding the return of the Jewish population held captive in Babylon for 70 years. Remarkably, Josephus the historian records for us that Cyrus read the Isaiah prophecy about himself and followed this up with a decree. Based on Cyrus' official decree, successor kings permitted the rebuilding of the Jerusalem Temple and city walls.

Cyrus was a secular shepherd, the anointed ruler, selected by God, as an answer to the prayers of God's people. He set in motion 50 years of national recovery for Israel.

Cyrus My Anointed

Even with a degree in theology, I have to admit that this Isaiah 45 scripture was taking me into some strange theological territory. I've never heard anyone teach that God actually raises up "anointed" secular shepherds, but the language from the Bible was clear.

I began reading further back in Isaiah and found this: *"When I say of Cyrus, 'He is my shepherd,' he will certainly do as I say. He will command, 'Rebuild Jerusalem'; he will say, 'Restore the Temple'"* (Isaiah 44:27-28, NLT). Cyrus, a secular ruler and a non-Jew, was not only anointed, but God also called him "My shepherd!"

The idea of Trump being an Isaiah 45 "Cyrus" archetype was intriguing to me. The word "anointed" in Hebrew denotes a person "specifically chosen and set apart for a specific task."

The puzzle pieces were starting to come together in a strange way. I went back to study Daniel and rediscovered the spiritual warfare he engaged in for 21 days (Daniel 10:13). That period culminated in a meeting with the archangel Gabriel who, fresh from battle with the "Prince of Persia," revealed that his warfare in the heavenlies was needed to shift and confirm leaders like Cyrus and Darius in office (Daniel 11:1). Daniel's account explains why there is spiritual warfare over certain elections and Supreme Court appointments. It explains what is happening even now in the United States!

Remember, at the time I heard this word, there were 17 candidates running to be the Republican nominee. Evangelicals were searching for the best conservative Christian candidate capable of beating Hillary Clinton. Many were leaning toward Senator Marco Rubio or Senator Ted Cruz. Others were attracted to Dr. Ben Carson, or the former pastor, Governor Mike Huckabee. All were running as clear-eyed conservative evangelicals, so why would God be talking about a secular ruler named Cyrus? Could Trump be God's Cyrus?

Think about it. How else would you describe a modern day Abraham Lincoln, Winston Churchill, Margaret Thatcher or Ronald Reagan? These leaders were not men or women who emerged out of the church—they were "Cyrus" leaders. It is only in retrospect that we canonize them and see the hand of Providence in raising them up to deal with the crises of their times.

In fact, Harry Truman was a "Cyrus" and even called himself that. As president, in 1948, he played a decisive role in making Israel a nation. Paul Charles Merkley of *Christianity Today* tells this story of President Truman:

> A few months after leaving office Truman was brought
> to the Jewish Theological Seminary in New York to meet

a group of Jewish dignitaries. Accompanying him was his good friend Eddie Jacobson, a comrade from his Army days and former business partner. Jacobson introduced his friend to the assembled theologians: 'This is the man who helped create the State of Israel.' Truman retorted, 'What do you mean, "helped to create"? I am Cyrus. I am Cyrus.' He knew the biblical story and understood his role in modern history.[11]

The Power of a "Cyrus Decree!"

The reason for the spiritual warfare becomes further evident when you see what Cyrus did. This secular ruler not only ended a period of prolonged spiritual deterioration, but he also authorized a spiritual release that ended a cycle of spiritual stagnation and captivity.

There are some interesting Bible characters who overlapped through this period. Daniel, Jeremiah and Ezekiel were all contemporary prophets at one point. Much of their prophecies and intercession concerned events that were not in their time and were stored up in the heavens for release. For instance, it was Jeremiah's prophecy about 70 years of captivity that prompted Daniel to pray for release. It was Daniel's prayer that set in motion the emergence of Cyrus and his decree.

Some of the things we pray and prophesy need to align with certain future events before they are released. Daniel did his part, but God had to put Cyrus in office to complete the equation. When the natural and spiritual realms line up, the pent-up bowls of intercession in heaven are tipped and things start to change.

The Cyrus decree, recorded in Ezra 1:1-4, is the moment Heaven authorized the return and restoration of God's people. The first phase involved rebuilding the house of the Lord. It was this "Cyrus decree" that worked its way through King Darius and King Artaxerxes until Nehemiah engaged his task to restore Jerusalem.

What About That Wall?

Trump's comments on "building the wall" have elicited all kinds of responses, but let's consider that perhaps this subject of "walls" in America involves something more. What do walls represent in the Bible? Proverbs 25:28 says, *"A man without self-control is like a city broken into and left without walls"* (ESV). America has become a country without walls—a nation without self-government.

We are out of control fiscally in Washington, physically at our borders, and morally in our values. On all points, our spiritual and natural gates are broken down. This is our Nehemiah project, to restore self-government and expose the folly of those who promise freedom while leading the nation into captivity.

What no foreign power could do, we have done to ourselves. It reminds me of a statement from Abraham Lincoln as he described circumstances of national unraveling preceding his own run for office. News then sounds like news today. Lincoln said:

> The increasing disregard for law, which pervades the country and accounts of outrages committed by mobs, form the every-day news of the times. At what point then, is the approach of danger to be expected? I answer, if it ever reaches us, it

must spring up amongst us. It cannot come from abroad. If destruction be our lot, we must ourselves be its author and finisher. As a nation of freemen, we must live through all time, or die by **suicide**.[12]

National suicide is the path that America is on, and the 2016 election will determine if that future can be altered. I believe it's the wrecking ball—Donald J. Trump—that has been sent to stop the momentum of this self-destruction. The Cyrus anointing is to build and restore.

Consider Modern Day America!

How long have Christians been praying for revival and awakening in our land? We have three decades of prayer and fasting and prophesying over America stored up and waiting for release! There has been extensive labor to bring reconciliation between races and the first peoples of this land. In spite of that, what we have witnessed nationally for the last eight years is nothing but erosion. Debt doubled. Race riots. Terrorism multiplied. Marriage redefined. It has been an agonizing unraveling descent into Babylon where modern kings lift their goblets in praise of themselves and their progressive achievements.

Your Role in 2016-2020

No politician can do the task that has been given to the American church—the task that we alone have the authority to carry out. The gates of hell will not yield an inch just because of a ballot box. In this American unraveling we need both a unified church and a Cyrus leader in government who is built to navigate the chaos—*a chaos candidate.*

I believe Trump is the chaos candidate who has been set apart by God to navigate us through the chaos coming to America. I think America is due for a shaking regardless of whom is in office. I believe the 45th president is meant to be an Isaiah 45 Cyrus. With him in office, we will have authority in the Spirit to build the house of the Lord and restore the crumbling walls that separate us from cultural collapse. Yet even then, this national project is likely to be done as Daniel prophesied: "*in troublous times*" (Daniel 9:25)

More than any other candidate in history, Donald Trump is receptive to what the church can do. If you think about it, no candidate other than Trump would even risk the political liability of promoting a faith-based solution to a problem, especially if they ran as an evangelical Christian. Can't you see them jumping all over President Cruz or Huckabee if one of them started pushing "faith based" initiatives? With Trump it's a different story. No one thinks he's a Christian so nobody suspects him of trying to push religion on people. At the same time, Trump is not embarrassed about his "Christianity." Who else would have taken on Pope Francis and said, "I am a Christian and I'm proud of it"? While not a line calculated to help him with Catholic votes, Cyrus Trump may challenge all Christians, including Catholics and Protestants, to public service. If people of faith have a solution that works, this man will be interested in seeing it.

Trump isn't nervous about Christianity. Through his journey, surrounded by African-American clergy and white evangelicals like V.P. nominee Mike Pence, Trump has come to the conclusion that making America great involves, in words he used in a Detroit church, "Renewing the bonds of trust between citizens and the bonds of faith that make our nation strong." Trump has come to the amazing and underpublicized conclusion that, "America's been lifted out of many of its most difficult hours through the miracle of faith. Now, in these hard times for our country, let us turn again to our Christian heritage to lift up the soul of our nation."

Why Is Trump God's Chaos Candidate?

I have a theory. As the world's lone superpower, America has been a nation singularly blessed by God in freedom, prosperity and peace. Indeed, we have proven the promise: *"Blessed is that nation whose God is the Lord"* (Psalms 33:12). We were once a nation that honored God, not necessarily as a Christian nation, but as a nation with a respect for Christ and appreciation for Christian influence in our heritage. That disposition has changed. (I'll share about this in Chapter 3.)

Trump once told a group of us that met with him: "If you don't mind me saying so you've gotten soft." From Trump's perspective, Christian leadership has become fearful of criticism and worried about confrontation. We have backed up and surrendered ground. Ministers want to avoid controversy. Controversy leads to loss of people and offerings. Many fear IRS backlash. In short, we have put ourselves into the very place Jesus warned about when he said that salt loses its savor and *"becomes trodden under foot of men"* (Matthew 5:13).

"Why," I asked, "did God not answer the prayers of His people by providing an experienced conservative Christian as a front runner?"

The answer seems clear now. I think it's an issue of stewardship. There is not a problem in America that could not be changed, if the Christian community actually showed up to vote. Did you know that there are 100 million born-again Christians in America?[13] Of this number, only 50 million are registered to vote. Of these 50 million only 25 million show up to vote, and these 25 million are often confused about who to vote for! We have been given a blessed land, but most Christians are too lazy or self-absorbed to steward the garden. Progressives, on the other hand, live, eat and sleep to accomplish their vision of creating a "utopia" on earth. There's no path to Eden without Christ—but that's not stopping them. Don't think you can hide. YOU are an impediment to their agenda. In the end they are coming for you—Hillary's basket of "deplorables." What's troublesome is that many liberals don't like each other, but they are willing to work together for their collective cause, while we Christians on the opposite side like each other but refuse to work together. By virtue of their philosophy, liberals are collectivists, so it's easy to pull everybody together to work. You'll see abortionists working on labor policy. You've got labor unions working on environmental policy. Conservatives, by virtue of their philosophy, are individualists. They create an organization to protect against gun control, but you can't get the gun owners to work against abortions and churches won't work with each other.

GOD'S PLAN ISN'T ALWAYS WHAT GOD'S PEOPLE CHOOSE

That's going to have to change.

The most troubling aspect of all this is the fact that God's plan isn't always what God's people choose. Just because Trump is a Cyrus doesn't mean the people can't end up rejecting him. God never told me Trump would win. He told me

Trump is a Cyrus for our nation if we have eyes to see. My burden is to get the church to see!

Either way, on November 9—the morning after Election Day—the nation will wake up divided like it hasn't been since 1860. This book explains what's happening.

So here is my theory:

> We, the people of God, have let the nation drift. Because we have not engaged our primary assignment of discipling our own nation, God is doing something that none of us expected. God has not left us. He continues to walk with this nation that once honored Him but now disregards Him by choosing a man who has not known Him to reveal Himself to him in the crucible of service. By choosing a man that has not know Him, to meet Him, and shape him in the crucible it is likely the nation will be shaped in the same manner also.

God is at work. He is indeed making a statement by what He is doing. We may be watching a prophetic sign in Trump that applies to all of us. Trump, the self-made man who can "get it done," enters the arena, and through the pressure of circumstance becomes the God-shaped man God enables to do what he could never do in his own strength.

The future of America is quite literally in our hands. History will happen in a matter of days. Will we show up or will we miss this moment? I believe the church in America will decide this vote.

Please freely share this chapter with others!
www.GODSCHAOSCANDIDATE.com

In the next chapter, I will take you to the moment Trump made the choice to run. You will be surprised who was used to get him to act.

Endnotes

1.   Retrieved from http://www.cnn.com/videos/politics/2015/12/15/jeb-bush-donald-trump-cnn-gop-debate-chaos-candidate-muslims-isis-12.cnn.

2.   Retrieved from https://www.amazon.com/Shadow-Party-Hillary-Radicals-Democratic/dp/1595551034.

3.   Retrieved from http://www.rushlimbaugh.com/daily/2007/03/16/eib_interview_tom_delay.

4.   Retrieved from http:// www.discoverthenetworks.org/individualProfile.asp?indid=977.

5.   Limbaugh Letter June 2015, Kirsten Powers Interview. pg 7

6.   Retrieved from https://books.google.com/books?id=m1joAgAAQBAJ&pg.

7.   Retrieved from http://www.abrahamlincolnonline.org/lincoln/speeches/gettysburg.htm.

8.   Retrieved from http://www.washingtonexaminer.com/its-the-supreme-court-stupid/article/2598256.

9.   Retrieved from http://www.breitbart.com/2016-presidential-race/2016/07/22/75-percent-positive-response-to-donald-trump-speech-so-cnn-trashes-its-own-poll/.

10. Retrieved from http://www.wsj.com/articles/u-s-seen-on-wrong-track-by-nearly-three-quarters-of-voters-1468760580.

11. Retrieved from http://www.christianitytoday.com/history/issues/issue-99/i-am-cyrus.html.

12. Retrieved from http://www.abrahamlincolnonline.org/lincoln/speeches/lyceum.htm.

13. Retrieved from http://www.gallup.com/poll/20242/Another-Look-Evangelicals-America-Today.aspx.

CHAPTER 2

THE CAMPAIGN BEGINS

In 2004, America began watching "The Donald," master of brand image, play the role of president every time he sat down on the set of *The Apprentice*. Trump performed the part as CEO of Trump Enterprises with this presidential image in mind. *The Apprentice* was where he unpacked his "America needs to get tough" message and delivered his *"You're fired!"* line, etching it into the American pop culture psyche. The truth is that Trump ad-libbed the line *"You're fired!"* It wasn't in the original script. The producer, however, agreed with Trump that it worked perfectly for the show. Trump never once recalled using those exact words, *"You're fired,"* in his real life career.

In fact, Trump's corporate culture is the opposite of the competitive and cut-throat antics seen on this television show. If you talk to his employees, male or female, you'll discover that none of them see him as a corporate Darth Vader checking up on the money-making efficiency of his starships. When he talks about building "great companies," he is not only talking about the balance sheet, but also the company culture. To his employees, Trump is viewed more as a patriarch than a prima donna. Most people miss this. Employee loyalty and longevity is high in the Trump organization.

While *The Apprentice* continued to keep Trump's brand image public, he published a book in 2011 on what he believed America needed most. The title of the book is *Time to Get Tough,* and it tested the public's reaction to his approach to solving America's problems. The response was as expected—more calls for him to run for public office.

In 2013, Trump conducted additional private research about a presidential run, but he remained hesitant. The timing was not right. Later that year, after speaking at the Conservative Political Action Conference (CPAC), he came home confident that he not only understood the pulse of the nation but also knew how to connect with it.

With all the research and data complete, it was actually over dinner one evening that he made the decision to run for president. While watching the evening news with his wife, Melania, they witnessed the escalating violence and riots happening in Baltimore. In that moment, Melania turned to Trump and said, "If you run now, you will be president."

"What?" Trump was legitimately shocked by this sudden declaration. "I thought you said I was too bright and brash to get elected?" She turned back to the plasma screen and said, "Something has changed. They are ready for you now."

Those words from Melania, especially **"You will be president,"** were spoken at just the right time, dissolving any hesitancy. Everything in his world was about to change. He could see it: "America doesn't have another election cycle left on the clock to correct the course."

The first thing Trump did was send a message to his attorney and Vice President of Trump Enterprises, Michael Cohen. Trump had already been through the process of pruning back future commitments. His reluctance to continue with the next season of *The Apprentice* was already making the network nervous. He directed Cohen to cancel his renewal on *The Apprentice* and move forward with the filing process as a candidate for the Republican nomination.

For a time, Trump's ambition to be president was known only by his close friends and family.

When filing the papers to run as a candidate for the Republican nomination, applicants must write a brief statement about their vision for the party. In his 2011 book, *Time to get Tough*, Trump selected the subtitle, "Making America #1 Again." For his campaign, as he travelled and spoke with constituents, his vision began to change. He penned, "To make America prosperous again, to make America strong again ... to make America great again."

Trump, the expert at branding and media, looked at what he wrote, "Make America great again." On June 16, 2015, he filed the paperwork to run for president of the United States, and those four words, "Make America great again," would define the core of his message.

The Early Trump

Trump's first chapter of life often confuses people, especially some believers. His world was that of a disciplined, but driven, deal-making, playboy billionaire. Somewhere, in his post-Marla Maples phase, he testified to having witnessed the seeds of self-destruction in himself. When his brother Fred tragically lost his life prematurely, Trump made the decision to swear off smoking, drinking and drugs of any kind. Even after that, he saw tendencies in himself that needed to be reined in and he decided to make some personal adjustments.

Let's be honest. Both presidential candidates in 2016 are flawed. But what makes Trump a specific challenge for Christians are the questions about his character. They don't like certain things he said or did in the past. Or they focus on the fact that he is now in his third marriage.

I can help you with that: you never judge an entire book by a single chapter. You have to read all the chapters to understand the

NEVER JUDGE AN ENTIRE BOOK BY A SINGLE CHAPTER

book. I once knew a man who had a great call on his life and was involved in politics, but he engaged in an affair with a married woman and got her pregnant. She insisted on keeping the child so he, fearing a public scandal, put together a scheme. Her husband was in the armed services so this man used his military connections to get her husband killed in combat. After things quieted down, he married the woman. When the story was exposed, it was a huge scandal. Most people who hear about this account assume the man left office in disgrace and went to prison. But he didn't. His name was King David. While this was a bad chapter—a disastrous chapter—in his life, it evidently wasn't the only chapter. God dealt with him. He paid a price for what happened, but when he came to his senses he repented and changed.

The ability to humble yourself and change is the quality God wants. That might explain the enduring affection God has for this guy named David and perhaps Donald also.

The Left is putting tens of millions of dollars into targeting women and evangelicals in particular with as much bawdy Trump data as they can find in order to build the narrative that both candidates are flawed so you might as well stay at home and not vote. The strategy is to suppress evangelical voter turnout.

The truth is, Trump is easy to defend if you understand his three chapters of life.

Again, no life should be judged by one chapter—you need to read the entire book. Trump's life is three chapters:

- **Chapter 1: Trump Starts** (1946 to 1977). This was the period of his youth, military school, the Wharton School of Business, working with his father and building his business.

- **Chapter 2: Billionaire Growing Up** (1977 to 2004). This chapter starts with his marriage to Ivana in 1977, and it ends with his divorce from Marla Maples in 1999. Trump had been married to Ivana when he met Marla. His second marriage was built on a flawed foundation. When his second marriage failed, he began his personal reckoning. After the divorce with Marla he made an assessment of his life. The death of his brother, Fred Jr., from alcoholism at 42 made an impression on him. Trump loved growing the business and in business matters was disciplined and driven. He already had sworn off drugs, cigarettes and alcohol, but he saw the seeds of destruction within himself in other ways. Trump was focusing on his children more. It was time to stop running around. From 2000 to 2004, Trump got grounded. He met Melania in 1998, got engaged in 2004, and got married on January 22, 2005.

- **Chapter 3: Trump Grown Up** (2004 on). This is the chapter where Trump did his best work as a father and husband. He also became more circumspect about what he said in public interviews. This third chapter of Trump's life is the one you should look at, as it is the third chapter that is the most revealing about who he is.

So when you hear criticism of Trump, or run into older quotes from Howard Stern interviews, remember it is the post-Marla Maples Trump who reformed. By 2004, he had made some major adjustments. And when you see his children, don't miss the obvious. Few young people could be raised with such wealth and privilege and not self-destruct. Notice the family discipline and work ethic. Notice how the kids relate to their father. He may have flunked the husband test earlier, but he passed the father test. The nation needs some new founding fathers more than anything. And post-Marla Maples, Donald looks like he has finally figured out how to better fulfill his role as husband, so take all this into account.

How Will I Be Remembered?

In private, navigating life's successes and failures, Trump was preparing himself for something greater. I asked a Trump insider what it was that motivated him to trade the security and comfort of his opulent private life to embrace the rigors and abuse of the campaign trail. "Was it ego only?" I asked.

The answer was interesting. Instead of ego, it was a sense of calling and the realization of mortality. Trump was turning 69. If he really felt America was heading for a disaster, he believed he had to do something now.

Trump is part of a uniquely American phenomena among the billionaire class. Like Andrew Carnegie, John D. Rockefeller and Cornelius Vanderbilt, the first part of their career was dominated by a relentless quest to be the biggest, the best and the richest in their field. In later years, the question arose, "How will I be remembered?" The great industrialists closed out their lives with a desire to be known as great philanthropists. They wanted to be defined by the quality of their contribution and not by their prestige or wealth.

Trump recounted how he had been wrestling with the question of legacy. How would he be remembered? There are three big questions people ask in this chapter of life—and Trump was considering all of them.

- **Question 1:** *"Is this problem big enough and compelling enough for me to devote my life to? Does it keep me up at night?"* For Trump, growing his business was no longer as great a passion as American policy. He saw America as a vast, powerful corporation that was being mismanaged by incompetent CEOs posing as elected officials. He constantly mused to himself, "These guys are killing America."

- **Question 2:** *"Am I, among all other people, uniquely qualified and positioned to deal with this problem?"* To Trump, politics is about the art of persuasion—first with the people and then with peers and all parties with vested interests. It's about working to get the best negotiated deal. This, in his mind, was where he excelled.

- **Question 3:** *"Has my sense of identity, destiny, or history thrust me into this responsibility?"* Curiously, Trump did not start his journey with a sense of "destiny" as such. What he did have was a sense of mission connected somehow to his family, both living and departed. Many were surprised when after his initial primary wins he looked up, pointed and acknowledged his parents and departed family members—his older brother Fred, in particular, who died of alcohol abuse in his 40s. It was as if they were in some way present to see what Donald was doing.

Beyond his desire to make his life's work matter, there was something else gnawing at him. All that he had built for his family was threatened by the paralysis of politicians who lacked the courage to stop government waste and national debt.

Trump the businessman could see that the country he loved was en route to a total economic disaster ... and the clock was ticking. The national debt, already at $19 trillion, would reach $21-$22 trillion, and then the whole house of cards would come tumbling down. Trump was confident that no single politician—Democrat or Republican—would tackle this problem. It would be a career-ending move in politics. That kind of bold aggressive action would alienate every financial backer. Trump knew he would have to run as a man who didn't owe favors to rich patrons. If need be, he would use his personal wealth to fund his political mission.

After filing to run for president, Trump went back to his bookshelf to find the well-marked copy of a book by Senator Rick Santorum, *Blue Collar Conservatives: Recommitting to an America That Works*. It outlined a thesis that resonated with Trump who is, himself, a blue collar billionaire. He read again of how Reagan ran as a charismatic Republican leader who won an entire new voting block of "Reagan Democrats." He saw in himself a similar ability to inspire, though the more personal, caring side would not come out until later.

The secret to Trump's Republican victory would be simple: He had to gain the endorsement of the hard-working middle class whose most immediate problems were the lack of jobs and opportunity. He could lead a sweeping populist movement by combining the blue collar voting block with another massive Republican voting block—100 million potential evangelicals.

With this strategy in place and the campaign ready to kick off, he made a note to contact his preacher friend Paula White. That note went to a Tampa-based public relations firm that worked with Paula. The head of this firm had just heard me speak and added me to the list of evangelical leaders invited to meet with Donald Trump at Trump Towers. This meeting was my opportunity to get the measure of the man up close—and to write this book.

Trump, the inexperienced politician, was just starting to discover what a hornet's nest he was stepping into.

CHAPTER 3

THE BOARDROOM

I climbed out of my NYC taxi staring up at Trump Tower and paused to take in the impressive architectural marvel. The entrance is vintage Trump, merging marble and brass into a fusion resembling the grandeur of a cathedral with the bling of a casino.

As I walked through the revolving doors for my first meeting, I began fumbling for the invitation I received so I could present it to the security guards stationed at the elevator.

While in the lobby, I watched the eclectic company of celebrity preachers and pastors start to assemble. When the time came, the entire group was escorted to the 26th floor boardroom.

As we took our seats, I realized that most of us did not know each other personally prior to this meeting.

Suddenly, the doors opened and the man himself entered the room. It is not easily noticed on television that Trump is a big guy, and I don't just mean in terms of personality. He is physically tall, standing at 6 foot 3 inches. Then, add shoes and hair and he stands another inch and a half.

His personal one-on-one style is more friendly than the person you see on television or on a platform debate. During our meeting Trump was gracious, non-confrontational and surprisingly open. Unlike his public persona where you only hear his opinions, Trump in person combines an inquisitive mind with a decision making process that is one-part practical and one-part intuitive. Trump has a knack for carving out unconventional paths to outcomes that other people miss. This is how he got the nomination. It's how he got the Trump National Doral deal in Miami. He flew down, rented a room, set up a phone and went to work. In a week, he had closed a highly competitive deal because he improvised and moved forward while everyone else was getting organized. He has a strong power of "intentionality." If he sees it, he can improvise a path toward it. This explains his unconventional playbook to win the nomination.

The Donald Meets the Evangelicals

Prior to this meeting with Trump, I caught an interview where he was talking about his trip to Iowa, where he first met "evangelicals." When asked what he thought about them, he paused and replied, "Well, they're interesting." He sounded like he had encountered a rare bird species seldom seen in Manhattan.

Evangelical leaders take the candidate vetting process seriously. But as a group, we are almost impossible to bring into collective alignment. As Trump joined the fray, many preachers were already advocating for their guy, Senator Ted Cruz, Dr. Ben Carson, former Governor Mike

Huckabee or Senator Marco Rubio. Some already agreed to be state chairman for their guy. One thing all agreed upon was that this next election was critical for America and highly winnable with the right candidate.

As always, the evangelical preference was for a "born again," bona-fide conservative. Trump didn't fit this description, but this meeting was his effort to change that.

After a few platitudes and a brief meet-and-greet, we got down to business.

As leaders asked questions and made comments, Trump rolled with the flow of the conversation.

Like many CEOs, he possesses a built-in meter that separates superficial ideas from ideas with substance. He measures folks quickly, too. As individuals at the meeting spoke, he was reading them and weighing their relative power within the group.

The meeting grew intense at one point.

A Messianic rabbi sitting near me said to Trump, "Your comments don't always represent you in the best light. People want to know you have a presidential temperament. They want to know that you are the person they can trust." Trump puckered his lips in characteristic fashion, nodded thoughtfully, and said, "I hear you." When the conversation turned to some of the more heated moments of the campaign, Trump explained, "You know, people aren't aware of what is coming at me ... what I am responding to. Like the storm that broke out when I took a stand on immigration, it can get pretty vicious. You don't always know the backstory. I can say this: I never punch indiscriminately.

I'm a counter puncher … but I fully hear what you are saying. I know where you're coming from."

Several of us exchanged glances. There was no denial and no need to drill deeper on the subject. Equally, there was no flippant or disingenuous commitment to change. He would do as the occasion required—until he clinched the nomination. After that? I deduced he would do as the occasion required in order to win.

One African-American leader, Bishop Darrell Scott of Ohio, spoke up, "I wouldn't change a thing. Be you, and keep being consistent. That's what people like about you. You're not playing politics."

Trump looked around the boardroom table and laughed. "So you're saying, 'Don't change'? Well, that's interesting!"

Scott continued, "Right! People would see you change, and they would know it isn't you. You would start to look political and that would make you look like everyone else. Just BE YOU!"

Scott added, "I came here with an open mind. In my way of thinking there are three branches of government: legislative, executive and judicial. You are clearly gifted for the executive branch. That's what you do."

Trump responded, "Thank you for that. You know in real estate, everyone likes renderings of buildings. You know what they are?" Trump asked, and then went on to explain, "They are the elaborate sketches of the building. I'm not big on renderings. I like to see a photo of the finished project."

This statement reveals much about Trump. He gets an inner picture of what the finished product looks like. Once that picture is clear, he intuitively finds the path to make it manifest. He is results oriented.

For instance, where will the money come from for job creation in inner cities? Trump provided insight, "We can cut so much waste in government. So many duplicated agencies at the state and federal level. It's ridiculous." His comments revealed what was going on in his mind, and as he did, I could hear Trump the CEO speaking: Cut bloated government waste and redirect savings to building infrastructure and jobs. That's the first solution to inner city poverty.

I recall hearing Trump once slip, "I can make this company great again … I mean country." It was a curious Freudian moment. He thinks like a CEO, not a politician. Trump went on, "We can recapture so much income. This is what I'm good at. The U.S. trade deficit with China is $400 billion, Japan $70 billion, Mexico $50 billion. It's ridiculous."

Trump tells the Church, "You've Gotten Soft!"

As the meeting continued, I was surprised to find that Trump actually *knew* some of the TV preachers in the room. He had not met them in person, but he had watched their programs.

Trump casually shared, "I was going around the dial last night and ran into *Politically Incorrect*, which is the popular left wing HBO talk show hosted by liberal comedian Bill Maher. Trump went on, "It's amazing how antagonistic they are about people of faith. It was painful to watch … it wasn't always like this in America." Trump wasn't pandering. He was making an observation.

Turning to Jan Crouch of TBN, he asked, "This seems to have been going on for a while hasn't it?" As she concurred, we all agreed. "It's open season on Christians in particular," someone added.

Trump scanned the room and said, "I think we had such a long period of Christian consensus in our culture and we kind of got … spoiled. Is that the right word?"

Then, he turned the tables on us and said something shocking, "Every other ideological group in the country has a voice. If you don't mind me saying so, YOU GUYS HAVE GOTTEN SOFT."

Ouch! That's the line I won't forget.

Then, in a moment of self-editing, he corrected himself, "I mean, WE, we, myself included, we've had it easy as Christians for a long time in America. That's been changing."

I think what Trump was saying is that, from his perspective, Christian leaders are a people living in "fear" of backlash for having opinions.

> CHRISTIANS ARE LIVING IN FEAR OF BACKLASH FOR HAVING OPINIONS

What he said next hit me in a particularly striking way. He added, "People who identify themselves as 'Christian' probably make up the single largest constituency in the country, but there is absolutely no unity, no punch … not in political consensus or any other area I can see."

The Side of Trump He Doesn't Want You to See

Pastor Steve Munsey spoke up, "This is the first time I've met Mr. Trump, but I would like to share something many of you might want to know. A few years back our city hosted the Miss Universe pageant. Now, we are not an affluent city, so hosting this pageant was a big deal.

There was talk of moving it to another city, but Mr. Trump stayed firm on the decision to keep it in Indiana.

"On his way to the pageant, Mr. Trump's limousine broke down and the driver had to change the tire. He was having a problem and a motorist pulled over and took over the repair and changed the tire. Mr. Trump got out and thanked the man and asked for his name and address. Mr. Trump paid off that man's mortgage. That's the side of him you don't hear about."

Trump was quiet. One of the pastors said, "People need to hear more about this side of you."

Trump smiled and shook his head saying, "No. It would mess up my image."

There are a number of stories like this. One friend who was adamant in his support of Senator Ted Cruz sheepishly admitted that he did once meet Donald Trump. "I guess it's only fair I tell you the story," he added. This man was hosting a fundraising banquet for battered women at Trump's Mar-a-Lago facility in Florida. He told the story that "Trump happened to be at the hotel and walked into the banquet room to talk to the bartender and see how the event was going. My friend went up and greeted Trump who was curious about the nonprofit. They joked briefly about how the fund raising was going and that Trump should feel free to pledge support. Trump asked a few more questions, walked over to the bar and wrote out a check for $50,000."

Trump's attorney shared a story that Trump was watching *60 Minutes* and saw the plight of three families destroyed by Maytag when the factory moved from Iowa to Mexico. He was so moved he told the attorney to find out who the people were and to find out how he could help them. He helped all three families.

One family owned a pizzeria that was going broke. Trump paid off the outstanding debt on the pizzeria so it could keep operating. For another family he paid off the daughter's tuition to college. In a third instance, a man's company was going broke but he had a product Trump liked. Trump Enterprises became the man's main customer and put him and his business back on their feet.

You will find story after story of Trump's intervention to bless others. And you wonder why he has favor? This is the side of Trump his family and friends know but that he keeps hidden from the public.

"Say Something!"

As the meeting drew to a close I had played the part of silent observer. Someone mentioned that CNN and FOX were in the lobby waiting to grab people for interviews after our meeting concluded. For some reason I was feeling a bit overwhelmed being in the boardroom with Trump and all the leaders present. The truth is, I was uncharacteristically playing small. I felt someone kick my chair. The man sitting behind me was the public relations agent who added my name to the list of key evangelicals. When I met him in the lobby earlier, he told me, "You've got something to add." When he kicked my chair, he leaned in and said, "Say something."

As Trump stopped speaking, I spoke out something a friend of mine named Marc Nuttle told me: "You know there is an important niche that no candidate has tapped into. As a businessman you are a natural to grab this demographic. There are 30 million small businesses in the

United States. They account for 70 percent of the economy and half the workforce. Small businesses are still the backbone of the U.S. economy. This includes 2.3 million Hispanic-American-owned businesses and 2 million of these are African-American-owned businesses. According to our data, a third of these 30 million businesses—a full 10 million of them—are companies family-owned by people of faith, the Christian community."

I continued, "All told, these 30 million small businesses represent about 100 million jobs and votes. No Republican candidate has ever gone after this huge opportunity."

I could see immediately that this wasn't an idea that electrified anyone. The clergy were primarily interested in social issues. Trump nodded. He was familiar with the data but did not grab the point either. His focus on the campaign trail would be blue collar voters and the opportunity to convert the Democrat working class to his cause. Small business wasn't his target.

Oh well, I thought, *at least I said something.*

When the meeting adjourned, Bishop Darrell Scott approached me. He saw the economic implications of what I said about the African-American community. We exchanged phone numbers.

Trump and the ministers went to the lobby to meet with reporters, but I hung back in the boardroom to check out the lunch table that no one had touched.

I said to myself, *Can you imagine the quality lunch Mr. Trump has catered at Trump Towers?* As I sampled the best sandwich wraps I have eaten in years, I noticed there was only one other guy in the room and he went back to the table as well. I heard him use some colorful language and was curious. "What ministry are you with?" I asked.

He laughed. "Me? Ha. Oh I'm not one of the clergy. I'm Jewish! I'm with Mr. Trump." He handed me his card. It was Michael Cohen, Trump's personal attorney and vice president of Trump Enterprises. "By the way," he said, "your numbers were right on." As I looked at his card, I explained that part of my lineage are Cohens who immigrated to the United States from Germany. "For all I know, we're related."

I gave him my card and he looked at it, "Wallnau, that doesn't sound Jewish."

"I know," I said, chuckling to myself. "It gets complicated."

As I left Trump Towers, I wondered what this trip was really all about. I'm a firm believer that the Lord directs our steps but, for the life of me, I could not connect these dots.

When I arrived home, something unusual happened.

CHAPTER 4

"I'M NOT MICHAEL COHEN!"

After I arrived home in Dallas, I got a call from Bishop Darrell Scott, the pastor of New Spirit Revival Center in Cleveland, Ohio. Darrell was one of the key leaders who connected with my thinking about Trump focusing on the 2 million African-American small businesses. He invited me to join him for a meeting of African-American clergy with Trump during an Atlanta rally.

Breaking Rank for Real Change

Working with Trump came at a price for some of the black ministers. They told me they received a lot of toxic feedback from those that do not approve of clergy breaking rank with the Democratic Party. Bishop Scott, however, is undaunted by this. He sees a window of potential— real change—coming into view with Trump. He explained that the African-American church is the one anchor of stability and strength in America's most challenged cities. For many pastors who supported President Obama, it has been surprising to see so little done for the black community over the past eight years.

Democrats have failed them on one side of the aisle, and the traditional Republican Party has written off their votes. The result is nothing pivotal being done by either party. But many expressed hope in Trump at this meeting.

Why? For two reasons: (1) Trump is not your typical Republican, and (2) Bishop Scott and his peers are not your typical African-American clergy. This is a story worth telling.

As Bishop Scott and I talked about the potential of real "faith-based initiatives" in restoring communities, I felt our hearts join. Isn't that like Jesus? Only Jesus can take two men who just met—one white and one black—and join them with one heart, for one cause, in one conversation. Bishop Scott wants Trump to revisit the faith-based concept applied to the most helpless war torn inner cities.

2016. The New Alliance Meeting. Rev. Dr. Scott, D., Dr. Wallnau, L.

Since Trump was already scheduled to go to the Atlanta Trade Center on Saturday, I was invited to join. Bishop Scott invited approximately 50 African-American ministers to meet with Trump prior to a press conference and rally.

Off I went. I arrived at the Atlanta Trade Center at 10:00 a.m. on Saturday morning. It was my first Trump rally and the crowds were coming in, soon to swell to 10,000 people. There I was, the lone white guy among 30 or 40 African-American clergy and their wives, all invited by Bishop Scott.

Before I knew it, I was pulled in front of a camera that introduced me as, "The architect behind the Trump organization, Mr. Trump's executive vice president and special counsel—his lawyer, Michael Cohen!"

The reporter then handed me a microphone. I stood there awkwardly frozen for a moment realizing they had confused me with Trump's attorney. There on live television I explained (in a Jerry Seinfeldian voice), "I'm not Michael Cohen, I'm Lance Wallnau. I'm with the clergy meeting with Mr. Trump."

Being the sole white guy—with some Jewish background—must have confused the man interviewing me. The fact that I just met Michael Cohen made the experience all the more surreal.

The interviewer motioned with his hand and said, "Say something."

Before I could think, I blurted out, "Donald Trump is a wrecking ball to the spirit of political correctness. Thank you," and handed the microphone back. Somebody else stepped in and continued talking.

In the next moment, I was whisked to an area constructed of blue curtains fixed to a temporary frame, like an Arabian tent inside the arena. Here, with about 75 African-American clergy, we took seats waiting to meet with Trump. We were so close to the stage area it was difficult to talk because of the loud music. Herman Cain was getting ready to speak.

The Trump Whirlwind

The moment Trump came through the door, the whirlwind came with him: security, media and staff all rushed into our curtained room. Trump warmly greeted the pastors and thanked them for coming to meet with him prior to speaking. He apologized for the tight schedule and rushed time with them. Not having a microphone, he waved his arms and invited everyone to come up, close like a football huddle. He threw his arms around the men near him and repeated his appreciation for the reception and told them, "It means a lot to me." Then, he pointed out that he had to go next door and do an impromptu media event for MSNBC, ABC and other networks.

Trump, who does not work with a teleprompter, simply improvised the next moment, much to the consternation of his security detail. "What do you say we do this together? You all come with me and stand with me on the platform."

The next moment was interesting. We went into the media room, only instead of being in the audience, we were in front of the cameras facing journalists with Trump. I slipped off to the side and took a picture of my new friends standing with Trump.

Donald Trump in the Media Room Surrounded by Pastors and Clergy

"This is a great group of friends of ours," Trump said. Trump told the confused press corps that the appearance wasn't planned.

"We just happened to be in another room, and I said, 'Come on, let's see the press,'" Trump said. "I actually like them much better than the media."

Trump immediately dragged Bishop Scott in front of the microphone! With his Trump hat on, the Bishop spoke about being encouraged by Trump's relationship with him and his receptivity to wisdom, prayer and the other leaders. "I don't know what type of legislator he would be," said the Bishop Scott, "but I know one thing, Donald Trump is a chief executive. He's a heck of a guy."

Then Trump drafted a startled friend of Bishop Scott's who, ready or not, was up next! Here's what Fox News reported: "Bishop George Bloomer, from Durham, N.C. Bishop Bloomer suggested that his connection to Trump and his bold campaign rhetoric is 'a spiritual thing.'" He spoke about the "scripture" and "about fire as a purifying and consuming thing." He said, "Fire tests and reveals what it comes in contact with. We need a consuming fire in this nation. Some things need to be removed. It's time for us to have somebody to bring jobs to this nation and (who will) look out for the Christians."

Trump's response was as I've seen with other spiritual moments in his life—revealing. He actually enjoys Pentecostal-type preachers. He wasn't entirely sure what the preacher meant about "fire," but what he understood he loved. "Wow. Was that awesome? What can you say after that! That was terrific."

Mr. Trump grew up as a Presbyterian under the popular Norman Vincent Peale, whose book, *The Power Of Positive Thinking,* was a lot different than what these men preach. Even so, Trump genuinely resonates with the African-American preachers. Bishop Scott suggested Trump see their houses of worship and meet their parishioners. Trump said, "Yeah, I got to do that," and he has been focusing on them intentionally during the critical last weeks of his campaign.

The press corps immediately went to work with their questions. Trump gave familiar answers and some amusing ones.

"Mr. Trump, how do you explain your success?"

Trump replied, "I attribute it all to my good looks."

They tried to bait him with a quote from Senator Ted Cruz who said he believed he would beat Donald Trump. "What is he supposed to say?" Donald asked them. "He has to say that. I don't consider that an attack."

The crowds were ready for Trump so he waved goodbye and took off for the stage.

He Knows It Is Going to Get Rough

Trump thrives on the crowd, saying, "These meetings energize me. There's like so much, what is it? It's like a lovefest. I can't explain it. You can feel the love. These meetings aren't negative—in fact they're very positive." He points to the news teams in the back of the room on scaffolding: "We even have the news media! Let's greet them."

The crowd immediately turns in mass and "boos" on cue. Many start to laugh and boo at the same time. It's sort of like the *Rocky Horror Picture Show*, a 1975 British musical comedy cult cinema experience where the audience gets up and interacts with the movie. The crowd was ready, waiting for its cue to participate.

"They never report the crowds. Go ahead. Scan the crowd!" The cameras all stay fixed and defiant. "What did I tell you? They never show the crowds. So dishonest."

The audience and Trump are having a good time, and booed again.

"But I have to tell you ... get ready folks," he warned his cheering audience. "The distortions of the news media and hundreds of millions of dollars in attack ads are coming. Who knows how much damage they will do."

You got the impression that Trump knew he was entering the toughest part of his campaign. All media guns were on him. But even as that took place, one unlikely group of pastors in the African-American community were reaching back to Trump to help him build a bridge.

CHAPTER 5

THEN I HEARD THE WORDS, "COMMON GRACE!"

I flew home from Atlanta and was updating some random social media activity when I ran across that picture of Trump I referred to earlier. It was Trump seated in the oval office with the words, *"Donald Trump 45th President of the United States."* I was dazed. Literally no one was thinking this would be a possibility, but I was sensing that this was more than some random Facebook meme—it was a prophetic picture of a real possibility. It struck me the same way the "wrecking ball" word had.

This is when I heard the Lord say, "Read Isaiah 45." I already shared about the word of Cyrus, but what I didn't share is the second part of that experience. After I read Isaiah 45 about *"Cyrus my anointed,"* two words echoed in my head: "Common grace … common grace!" I had just run across that term a few weeks earlier. This is a term used by Reformed Theologians that was first introduced to me while reading Chuck Colson—the 1970's Nixon-era political strategist who pleaded guilty to obstructing justice, served seven months in prison, was born again and founded a worldwide prison ministry. Ever wonder what keeps fallen man from total self-destruction?

Common grace comes down upon a fallen world to keep the forces of anarchy in check. It stirs in man the ideals of virtue and justice. It is the grace that comes upon all, Christian and non-Christian, to help us affirm the good and resist the bad, personally, and within institutions. It is the hidden hand of God that works to promote justice and order in a world where selfishness could produce societal collapse. "Saving grace" is what gets you saved. "Common grace" is the special influence of God that comes upon man to keep society from imploding.

I liked Trump earlier, but in my first meeting with him, I was wanting to hear a "saving grace" testimony. After thinking it through, I realized that "common grace" anoints men and women for an assignment that may make them more qualified than my favorite "saving grace" Christian.

As I read Isaiah 45, a verse jumped out at me: *"I have even called you by your name; I have named you, <u>though you have not known me</u>"* (Isaiah 45:5).

Have not known me? Suddenly, I felt better about Trump.

"Common Grace" Raises Up Unpredictable Vessels

Trump falls into a unique category of individuals—men and women served up by the hand of Providence. They are people whose singular strengths and convictions match a certain test in history—a crucible. As Churchill said, "All my life was a preparation for this moment." Figures like Margaret Thatcher, George Patton, Winston Churchill and Abraham Lincoln do not step out of cathedrals onto the stage of history, yet we canonize them later as the instruments raised up by God to meet a singular crisis.

Curiously, many of these leaders were not the darling or favorite of contemporary Christians. Preachers thought Lincoln was a godless skeptic. They stumbled over Winston's cigars and scotch. They balked at Reagan's divorce and children from two marriages. Likewise, today, leading evangelicals have made their rejection of Trump public!

Strangely, while none of these instruments of "common grace" rose through the ranks of evangelicals—EACH of them ended up as a defender of Christian values.

This is the question you need to ask, especially when your favorite Christian candidate fails to get the nomination. Don't ask, "Who is the strongest believer running?" but, "Who is the one anointed for the task?"

Trump Has the Cyrus Anointing

"Common Grace" tells us that God acts in history in unusual ways to raise up unlikely deliverers for the sake of his purposes and his people. He disrupts nomination processes. In 1860, the pious evangelical Salmon P. Chase was a better Christian than the men he ran against, but the wily Lincoln got the nomination on the third ballot. Chase could not understand why God had denied him, but in the end the Springfield lawyer proved to be the most suitable vessel for the coming chaos.

From my perspective, there is a Cyrus anointing on Trump. He is, as my friend Kim Clement said three years ago, "God's Trumpet."

Once I heard the "Cyrus" word, I predicted openly that he would win the nomination.

People Keep Asking Me: "Is Trump a Christian?"

Not surprisingly, one of the greatest enemies Trump faces is the religious spirit. Prophets and preachers—and not a few business folks who make money from the left—have rejected Trump because of his past. Some have failed to discern who he is. Others have a vested interest in not seeing his growth or really hearing his proposals.

The spiritual transformation of Trump is interesting to watch if you know the whole story. He has had moments of private soul searching, humbling and encounters with anointed preachers.

It is a peculiar irony to me that Trump is accused of being racist, yet by my observation, his experience of Christianity has been most profoundly shaped by African-American clergy. His most recent visit to a church in Detroit reveals the metamorphosis taking place. He said:

> Please know this: For any who are hurting, things are going to turn around. Tomorrow will be better. It will be much better. The pastor and I were talking about riding up the street and we see all those closed stores and people sitting down on the sidewalk and no jobs and no activity. We'll get it turned around. We'll get it turned around, pastor. Believe me.
>
> We're going to win again as a country and we're going to win again for all of our people. I want to work with you to renew

the bonds of trust between citizens and the bonds of faith that make our nation strong.

America's been lifted out of many of its most difficult hours through the miracle of faith and through people like Bishop Jackson and Dr. Jackson.

Now, in these hard times for our country, let us turn again to our Christian heritage to lift up the soul of our nation. I am so deeply grateful to be here today and it is my prayer that America of tomorrow, and I mean that, the America of tomorrow will be one of unity, togetherness and peace, and perhaps we can add the word prosperity—OK, prosperity."

> LET US TURN AGAIN TO OUR CHRISTIAN HERITAGE TO LIFT UP THE SOUL OF OUR NATION

Let us also consider that as much as 70 percent of Americans self-describe as "Christians." These include Catholics, Presbyterians, Episcopalians and Lutherans. Within the total population, 30 percent say they have encountered Christ in a "born again" experience. There are many who believe they are Christians who do not use our language. Are they trying to deceive us? No.

In that first meeting with evangelicals, Trump exposed something about himself that I think you will find interesting. It was when he revealed how he views himself in contrast to pastors and clergy. Tapping his Bible, he said, "Look, I freely admit that while you all were pursuing a higher calling, I was running around building buildings and making money." It beckons back to an earlier time in American life when "men of the cloth" were held in higher esteem.

Notice that Trump considers the work of ministry a "higher calling" than what he was doing when he made his billions. In some ways, this was a humbler admission than many rich Christian donors would make.

Donald Trump may be shrewd, but in matters regarding his faith, he possesses the self-conscious candor of a man who knows he falls short, but who fundamentally shares the same beliefs.

In Search of the Perfect Christian President

It has gradually dawned on evangelicals that having the right person in the Oval Office may be more important than voting their favorite Christian. Remember Jimmy Carter? We all got excited when the governor became the first candidate to run as a "born again" Christian. How did that work out? When the twice-married Ronald Reagan ran for office, he needed help from Jerry Falwell Sr., who reminded believers that they weren't voting for a national pastor but a president. *The New York Times* mocked Reagan as badly as they mock Trump today. Reagan was described as a "Grade B" actor and cowboy. In the end, Ronald Reagan became the gold standard for every Republican after him.

George W. Bush was a Christian who credited Billy Graham with helping him find faith. He got support from evangelicals who made a decisive difference in his close election with Al Gore. In retrospect, after seeing the outcome of going into Iraq, the increase of government debt—more than any President other than President Obama—and the 2008 financial collapse, one wonders if the only question Evangelicals should ask is, "Does he know the Lord?" Or, to phrase it differently, if you were cauth in a storm and needed to fly through it safely, would you rather have an inexperience pilot who happens to be a Christian, or an experienced pilot who doen't know the Lord?

Does Trump Pray?

Asked point blank, "Do you pray?" Trump hesitated only a moment and then said unapologetically and emphatically, "Yes, I do."

Trump is multifaceted, but not complex. He is genuine in seeking to honor God as he understands God. I don't think Trump is a choir boy, but I do believe he is genuine. My sense is that his relationship with God is a growing conversation inside his own heart as he feels the weight of what he is stepping into. In this sense, he reminds me of another historical character, Abraham Lincoln—a man revivalists were dubious about because he did not attend church regularly. Yet he was a man who had a center of gravity more aligned with God's principles than the pious Christians he was running against, like Samuel Chase.

What Lincoln had was a respect for the Bible and a deposit of Christian values from his mother. Curiously, Donald Trump's Bible was given to him in 1955, with a personal note from his mother on the inside cover. It was this Bible he tapped while talking to us.

A Prophetic Businessman

This will surprise some, but Trump is more prophetic than most people realize. I think great entrepreneurs—like Steve Jobs, for example—tend to be prophetic. Repeatedly, I have heard Trump say, "Leadership is all about seeing the future and not listening to the short-sighted thinker. This is the kind of leadership we need to turn this country around—and fast."

> LEADERSHIP IS ABOUT SEEING THE FUTURE

He repeats this phrase often: "Leadership is about seeing the future." He is Churchillian in this regard. He sees the threat no one else has courage to talk about until it's too late. He sees it with radical Islam, he sees it with the soaring debt and he sees it in America's tinderbox inner cities. He accurately predicted that Brussels was no longer the same community he knew years ago—his statement that was being picked apart by the press at the very moment Brussels became the epicenter of another round of organized terror and death. Likewise, Trump predicted the "Brexit," while expert commentators in media and government were stunned. Christians should take note of this. It's a curious contrast, Trump's prophetic foresight versus the Left who never see what's coming and are in denial after it comes to pass.

"I Don't Know That I Deserve it"

The genuineness of Trump's connection to evangelicals was on full display during the acceptance speech he delivered in Cleveland, where he thanked them and, in a rare moment of emotional vulnerability, spoke off-script saying, "I don't know that I deserve it." This one moment reveals the true heart of the man.

As mentioned before, the mainstream described Trump's message at the Republican National Convention in Cleveland as gloomy, pessimistic, and dark. However, those who agree with Trump found the message encouraging simply because someone was finally telling the truth! A full 73 percent of Americans say that the country is on the wrong track. Trump is very much like Churchill, raising a warning cry about the unraveling of America at a time when the ruling class, buttressed by the media, want to deny there is anything wrong! In all likelihood, Trump is intuiting that which is on the horizon if changes are not made. And, like Churchill, the opposition wants to exile him for sounding an alarm in his disturbingly blunt manner.

While it may be easy to understand the hatred against Trump that comes from people whose only impression of him is formed by liberal media, it is particularly painful to see evangelicals viciously attack him. They have a friend in Trump. It would be wise for believers to heed the words of Jesus, *"Let him alone, he that is not against us, is for us."* This is especially true if the one you are attacking is sent to help you.

CHAPTER 6

THE GOSPEL IN BLACK AND WHITE

When Bishop Darrell Scott was orchestrating a follow-up meeting at Trump Towers for African-American clergy, he gave me the dates and invited me to attend. He called right after I had the remarkable "Cyrus" discovery and told him about that and my discovery of "common grace." He fully got what I was trying to say.

Prior to this second visit to Trump Towers, Trump's rallies were being increasingly targeted by activists of various stripes, and the liberal media were keen to exploit a narrative that would place the blame on Trump. This next meeting would be significantly different than earlier meetings hosting mostly white evangelicals. This meeting was twice as large and mostly African-American. The next gathering would become the start of a National Diversity Coalition, now standing at 700,000 Americans.

An incident right before the meeting was exploding on the media with videos focused on the physical altercations happening at the event. The boardroom was packed with black clergy and spokespeople for various action networks. Government Secret Service and private security was increasing around headquarters since my last visit to Trump Towers. Those of us attending meetings were now individually scanned before gaining entry into the boardroom.

As Trump entered the room he paused and smiled. Holding the Bible—almost like a steering wheel—he said, "You know, normally I bring this Bible to meetings to show, but today I'm carrying it for protection!" Everyone laughed and the tension momentarily dissolved.

Trump took his seat at the head of the conference table next to Bishop Darrell Scott. I noted that Omarosa Manigault was also seated toward the front. I remembered her as the draconian female star of earlier episodes of *The Apprentice*. I discovered after this meeting that Manigault is a believer who wanted to personally be present to address any questions about Trump's racial history, because she is not only a business partner, but also someone he helped with a nonprofit library project that she introduced him to years earlier.

Bishop Scott opened the meeting and gave an impressive exhortation to set the context for the meeting. He began by sharing that he came as a man who grew up in the "hood" and understood the challenges of the inner city. As a pastor, he came to the political process looking for solutions.

He listed some hard statistics about the decline of African-Americans over the last eight years under current leadership. He said, "During this past administration there has been a 58 percent rise in African-Americans needing food stamps and a 20 percent increase in those not in the labor force. Race relations have deteriorated and frustration is mounting. Hard as it is to break rank with tradition," Scott explained, "the urgency of the hour and the frustration with progress in the African-American community forced me to seek God for new answers."

He explained that he came to know Trump a few years before he announced his candidacy. Scott is convinced that a political leader has finally emerged who sees America being torn apart by political incompetence, apathy and indifference. Scott said he knows racism when he meets it and knows for certain that Trump doesn't operate in that spirit. To him, "Donald Trump is a man uniquely gifted as a chief executive officer who can tackle the problems others avoid and, for once, change the status quo for the black community if given a chance. Trump is interested in America, not party politics. That's why I stand with this man."

Trump knew Scott before the meeting, but he never actually heard him as a speaker. He looked around the room and said he wished Scott's opening was recorded. "I mean it" Trump said. "I'd like to read that or hear it again. You really hit on something."

The conversation opened up and various people engaged in the give and take. Trump spoke up, "Look, we have a problem here and much of it relates to economics. When I saw what was happening in Ferguson [Missouri] and Baltimore, I was concerned. We have dozens of cities and communities in the same place."

The subject turned to the recent event where a video showed physical altercations between an African-American and security at a rally. One of the pastors told Trump, "There's no excuse for this. You have to show more Christian restraint in the way you handle these things. People should not be subjected to getting roughed up."

Trump responded. "Look, I hear you and I'm open to what you're saying. Let me ask you a question. How many of you here are preachers?"

Several gestured to him.

"Let me ask you. What would you do in your church if someone tried to take over the meeting while you were preaching? How do you handle that? Do you have elders or deacons or someone that steps in?"

From my vantage point, as an observer, what took place next was interesting. One preacher said, "I don't put up with that foolishness."

Another added, "Nobody takes my pulpit from me when I'm preaching."

A third said, "I'll tell you what, if somebody tries to physically take over my service, the last thing we're worried about is hurting their feelings. They'll be removed."

Trump replied, "That's what I'm talking about. We will try to do a better job of this. Nobody is singling anyone out. We're just trying to keep order and get on with our meeting."

I'm not sure what Trump did, but after that meeting he had no incidents that became tabloid material, and when he saw the possibility of physical violence threatening an upcoming rally in Chicago, he chose to cancel the event. At a rally in Arizona, where protesters blocked the highway and others surrounded the entrance, aerial coverage showed Trump and security climbing a path behind the venue to get in and conduct his meeting.

As we wrapped up our discussion, the room erupted in applause at one poignant moment when one of the clergy shared something that moved Trump: "In my church we don't preach a message based on grievances and handouts. We believe the Gospel of Jesus Christ proclaims a kingdom that has the ultimate power to lift any individual right out of the most impoverished circumstances. God's Word can empower anyone with the wisdom and ability to rise above any obstacle and succeed in life!"

GOD'S WORD CAN EMPOWER ANYONE WITH THE WISDOM AND ABILITY TO RISE ABOVE ANY OBSTACLE AND SUCCEED IN LIFE

Trump said, "Wow! I've never heard that before," as the room erupted in spontaneous "Amens" and applause.

As in the first trip to Trump Towers, this time the media was all set up in the lobby to ambush those attending. CNN, ABC, MSNBC, all the New York outlets, were waiting. Some quick decisions were being made about who would speak, but before we adjourned my dear friend, Bishop Darrell Scott, pointed across the room at me and said: "Before we go, I'd like Dr. Wallnau to share with Mr. Trump that word you told me yesterday about him."

I was sitting at the corner on the opposite end of the table, literally in the same seat I sat in for the last meeting when my chair got kicked and I was told to "say something."

I had shared everything with him. We had talked about the 45th president, and Isaiah 45, and Cyrus, and "Common Grace," and the fact that Isaiah says Cyrus "*is My anointed,*" and "*though you do not know me.*" I shot him back a nervous look and asked, "What part do you want me to share?"

He leaned back and with a sweeping gesture of his hand said, "All of it."

Lance Shares with Mr. Trump

I remembered that for some reason I had carried my Bible in my briefcase into the meeting. I reached down and put the Bible on the table and began to explain to Mr. Trump that, from my perspective, there were so many near misses that would have taken down another candidate, yet he somehow survived.

"I think at some point you have to see the grace of God on this."

I said he reminded me of George Washington, who had horses shot out from under him and bullets whizzing past, but he somehow survived. I shared Isaiah 45, and the word to Cyrus, and how I believe it applied to him. He nodded attentively, trying to understand what he could. I would have stopped there but Bishop Scott wanted the preachers in the room to know about "Common Grace," so I explained how God calls and empowers even those that "know him not." I explained he has much support in our tribe, yet we, who are evangelicals, don't base our support for him on the fact that he is one of us, but because of the grace of God that we see on him. We believe God has blessed him and God has his hand on Mr. Trump. As the meeting broke up, Mr. Trump came toward me and stood in front of me with his hands on his chest, saying, "What you said really, uh, how do I put it? It meant a lot to me. I mean that." In church language, he was saying that "what I said ministered to him."

Trump's Spiritual Journey— Discovering What Makes America Great

It is a peculiar irony that Trump is accused of being racist, yet he, more than any Republican before him, is making the African-American community his priority. Not surprisingly, his experience of Christianity has been most profoundly shaped by African-American clergy. His most recent visit to a church in Detroit on September 3, 2016, reveals the metamorphosis taking place in his own life. In the church, Trump laid out how the permanent "political class" on both sides has failed everyone in the United States including America's black communities.

Our political system has failed the people and works only to enrich itself. I want to reform that system so that it works for you, everyone in this room. I believe true reform can only come from outside the system. I really mean that. Being a businessman is much different than being a politician because I understand what is happening. And we are going outside the establishment.

Please know this: For any who are hurting, things are going to turn around. Tomorrow will be better; it will be much better. The pastor and I were talking about riding up the street and we see all those closed stores and people sitting down on the sidewalk and no jobs and no activity. We'll get it turned around. We'll get it turned around, pastor. Believe me.

We're going to win again as a country and we're going to win again for all of our people. I want to work with you to renew the bonds of trust between citizens and the bonds of faith that make our nation strong.

America's been lifted out of many of its most difficult hours through the miracle of faith and through people like Bishop Jackson and Dr. Jackson.

> AMERICA'S BEEN LIFTED OUT OF MANY OF ITS MOST DIFFICULT HOURS THROUGH THE MIRACLE OF FAITH

Now, in these hard times for our country, let us turn again to our Christian heritage to lift up the soul of our nation. I am so deeply grateful to be here today and it is my prayer that America of tomorrow, and I mean that, the America of tomorrow will be one of unity, togetherness and peace, and perhaps we can add the word prosperity—OK, prosperity.

Trump's message in Detroit reminded me of something Bishop Darrell Scott said in one of our meetings, "Looking back over the last 15-20 years, the closest thing to a breakthrough for the black community was the faith-based initiatives experiment under President George W. Bush. They never really looked at the data," Darrell said. "The early results were impressive and nothing since then has come close to tapping into the latent power of the African-American church to make a difference in these communities."

From this moment onward, Trump began wrestling more specifically with the challenges facing the African-American community. When riots broke out in August in Wisconsin, Trump began to make his case for how his administration would be different than previous Democrats or Republicans. Trump's legacy is about making America great again, and that includes all races and all socioeconomic backgrounds. It is not about making Republicans great.

The colorful fight promoter Don King has been a friend of Trump for years. Introducing Trump to a pastor's gathering at Bishop Scott's church in Cleveland, Ohio, King said, "My friend Donald Trump only sees one race, the human race." King pointed out the absurdity of media accusations portraying Trump as a "Hitler or KKK" when his history with black celebrities and entertainers spans 30 years of public record.

As our meeting ended, one minister asked a candid question: "So often, when evangelicals come behind a candidate, they are used for their vote and forgotten about afterward. I want to know if the door will still be open to you in the future or will we be forgotten?"

Trump paused, and spoke directly. "No. You *will* have access." The proof of this statement was played out clearly as the man who asked was invited to speak in prime time at the Republican Convention.

CHAPTER 7

THE CONVENTION

As thousands of people descended on Cleveland, Ohio, for the 2016 Republican National Convention, no one could have anticipated the circus that was about to erupt.

The evening of day three is always reserved for the nomination and acceptance speech of the vice presidential nominee. This was the moment for Donald Trump's pick for vice president, Indiana Governor Mike Pence, to make his mark. However, all eyes were instead on Senator Ted Cruz's speech that night.

To have cancelled Senator Cruz before he spoke would have provided a bombshell to the press and made Senator Cruz the focus of the convention. Trump decided to just let the drama play out.

The speech was cleared by Paul Manafort, Trump's campaign manager at 4:30 p.m. and programmed into the teleprompter. They understood Senator Cruz would not be endorsing Trump, which must have been a disappointment to Trump, who was doing all he could to unify and build party momentum at the convention. If reconciliation was possible, Trump was willing to move toward it as he had with Dr.

Ben Carson, Governor Chris Christie, Governor Mike Huckabee and top staffers from all the candidates—including Senator Cruz's.

In fact, up until a few hours before Senator Cruz's speech, the Trump campaign had been in negotiations with him about playing a larger role in the campaign, including advising on Israeli policy.[1]

When the time came for Senator Cruz to speak, the crowd was respectful and anticipated a unifying speech. They responded positively all the way up until they realized … Senator Cruz was not going to keep his pledge. He was not going to endorse the Republican nominee. To whatever extent possible, Cruz was going to keep his fist tightly clenched around the delegates he won.

Candidate Trump, standing in the back of the auditorium behind a curtain, listened as Senator Cruz made his statements. Trump's instincts told him to be prepared for anything the Senator might do or say.

Senator Cruz was winding up, "We deserve leaders who stand for principle, who unite us all behind shared values, who cast aside anger for love … and to those listening, please, don't stay home in November…"

APPLAUSE

The audience thinks he's messaging the #NeverTrump-ers to not sit out—waiting for the Senator to reveal his endorsement of Trump…. "If you love our country, and you love our children as much as I know that you do, stand and speak and vote your conscience…."

APPLAUSE CONTINUES

The audience is thinking he's messaging the #NeverTrump-ers—"Vote for candidates up and down the ticket, who you trust to defend our freedom and to defend the constitution ..."

Mic Drop

What?! The realization hit the live audience and millions at home. This is it?

There would be no endorsement from Senator Ted Cruz!

A chorus of "boos" began to build from the front of the audience where the New York delegation was located. They began to chant: "We want Trump, we want Trump, we want Trump!"

At this point, the senator quipped back, "I appreciate the enthusiasm of the New York delegation."

Slighting Trump's New York delegation at his own convention, was like putting a lit match to gasoline. The uproar of "boos" grew louder and louder until all corners of the arena echoed with "boos."

Senator Cruz lost the entire convention floor.

Trump's instincts served him right. He had positioned himself so that if anything unexpected happened, he could step in. As the crowd called for "Trump, Trump," he pulled aside the curtain and waved. Stepping out into the arena, he shifted the focus and distracted attention from Senator Cruz, who, amidst the uproar, finished his speech.

Covering this moment, Chris Matthews of MSNBC said, "The phrase 'vote your conscience, up and down the ticket,' that's political language for, 'I'm releasing you not to vote for the party.' I mean, he was saying to people in the Republican Convention, 'you don't have to vote Republican this time.' It was an incredible, I think outrageous, misuse of his time, but they gave him the time."[2]

Vice-presidential nominee Mike Pence, gracious fellow that he is, had to endure the media obsession with the Senator's speech. Hardly anyone remembered or quoted a line from Governor Pence that night.

Watching the mayhem, former House Speaker Newt Gingrich took the stage and, amid residual boos, attempting to paraphrase Ted Cruz's talk, he began to ad lib comments, ignoring the prepared script in the teleprompter.

"With no requirement for endorsement, Donald Trump generously encouraged his competitors to speak once again," he said. "Governor Rick Perry, Governor Chris Christie, Governor Scott Walker, Dr. Ben Carson, Senator Marco Rubio, and Senator Ted Cruz have all responded." Gingrich continued, "So, to paraphrase Ted Cruz, if you want to protect the Constitution of the United States, the only possible candidate this fall is the Trump-Pence Republican ticket."[3]

Speaking on Fox News to Sean Hannity right afterward, Gingrich said, "I had the text of what Ted Cruz was gonna say, and I thought it was funny. I mean, Ted gets up and he says, 'Look, vote your conscience for someone who will support the Constitution.' Well, in this particular election year, that by definition cannot be for Hillary Clinton. So in a very strange way, for a guy who's a Princeton Harvard graduate, he backed into ... he has to be for Trump, because by Ted Cruz's own standard, there's no other candidate that fits the criteria Ted Cruz set up."[4]

The Circus Master

Senator Ted Cruz knew what he was doing. His decision to close out the campaign this way was political calculus. He was, and is, banking on Trump failing in 2016. By distancing himself from Trump, and telling his party to "vote your conscience," he was positioning himself as the "courageous conscience" of the conservative cause in 2020.

> SENATOR TED CRUZ WAS BANKING ON TRUMP FAILING IN 2016

Ted, like other #NeverTrump conservatives, had not considered what would happen if Trump didn't lose to Hillary in a close election. The #NeverTrump conservatives will be marked and scorned as party saboteurs. The decision was bad math based on an unresolved personal offense.

Throughout the primary season, the team of Glenn Beck and Senator Ted Cruz convinced their audiences that November 2016 will be the most consequential election in American history, rivaled only by the Lincoln election of 1860. We were told our future as a nation is literally at stake. From the three to four appointments to the Supreme Court, to the $19 trillion deficit, time after time Beck and Senator Cruz made the argument that we cannot blow this election. No one who bought into that narrative took lightly Senator Cruz's decision to risk sabotaging Republican Party success.

How could Senator Cruz—the would be deliverer—withhold support when what was at stake is the very survival of the nation? It's doubtful that Ted was disingenuous on the campaign trail when he talked about what is at stake. The truth is that the arrows that flew in the nomination process found vulnerability in his armor. He was deeply and personally offended by Trump, and this wound led him to strike back—even if withholding support for the nominee was a detriment to the party and the nation.

Senator Ted Cruz, his wife and father are solid evangelicals. They are good people. Someone connected to Ted's team struck out at Melania Trump and provided salacious pictures from her modeling career in an effort to discredit Trump. Yes, Trump's team released equally inappropriate advertising about Ted's wife and father. This exchange went too far and hurt the family. Trump is a novice in the art of biblical reconciliation—but Ted and his father are not. While months later Ted said that he would vote for Trump, there was a unique opportunity to share the Gospel message, to practice forgiveness, and to reconcile with his Christian brother that was grossly missed during this exchange.

By letting evil overcome good, Senator Cruz allowed personal unforgiveness to take priority over the best interests of the nation at the time. His immediate response was to let the Republican Party learn its lesson and suffer the consequence of choosing Trump over a more principled man, like himself, who would be back in 2020.

In light of his unresolved feelings toward Trump, we can read between the lines in his speech to see what he is really saying. Look at the sentence right before he told people "not to stay home in November ..."

He said, "We deserve leaders who stand for principle, who unite us all behind shared values, who cast aside anger for love." He was implying that Trump is the anger candidate instead of love candidate, that he does not share conservative values and who does not have principles.

And Senator Cruz?

Well, he is the leader they deserve who will share their values and stand for principle—later.

The Kingdom Moment Ted Missed

I am not seeking to minimize the pain the Cruz family may have experienced or the nastiness in what Trump's team released in response to attacks on his wife, but I believe this is a huge "Aha!" moment for evangelicals.

If someone runs for office like Senator Cruz, as a Christian candidate seeking church support, it is assumed they are practicing their faith in a political public arena. Jesus taught, *"If your brother sins against you, go and tell him his fault, between you and him alone. If he listens to you, you have gained your brother"* (Matthew 18:15). Or, if you subscribe to the idea that this verse applies only to spiritual brothers and Trump is not a Christian, you could use this verse: *"And when you stand praying, if you hold anything against anyone, forgive them, so that your Father in heaven may forgive you your sins"* (Mark 11:25).

Cruz allowed unforgiveness and perhaps personal ambition to override honoring his word on his pledge to support whoever was nominated by the Republican Party. Why do I say that he allowed a personal unresolved offense to frame his strategy? This was made clear when addressing the Texas delegation at a breakfast the day after:

"I am not in the habit of supporting someone who attacks my wife and attacks my father ... That pledge [to endorse the eventual nominee] was not a blanket commitment that if you go and slander and attack Heidi, that I'm going to nonetheless come like a puppy dog and say, 'Thank you very much for maligning my wife and maligning my father.'"[5]

Perhaps this thin skin reveals something about Senator Cruz as a candidate—that God knew and we missed? Maybe God, who knows the hearts of all men, is still shaping Senator Cruz for an important future role. During the grueling vetting process all candidates go through, he had to disclose that in spite of his and his wife's earnings, he could "do a little better" in practicing Biblical disciplines such as tithing. Trump on the other hand is a closet philanthropist who likes to keep his generosity secret and a safe distance from his "time to get tough" public image.

What if Ted Cruz came to grips with his offense? Imagine him saying to his wife, "Heidi, Honey, I need to get this right. Will you go with me to meet with Donald and Melania? This man, if he becomes president, will need all the help he can get."

Now imagine Donald and Melania having a heart to heart talk with Senator Cruz briefly sharing what was going on and showing the Trumps this verse from Matthew on forgiveness in the Bible. What if Ted explained to Melania that though he did not know about the degrading advertising that targeted her as a smear tactic, he took personal responsibility for it and wanted to ask her forgiveness?

What if the Senator then asked Donald to forgive him for harboring such deep hatred for the way Heidi was treated? "I know there's a lot of give and take in rough campaigns, but this hit me differently. It became personal. I don't like the way I've been harboring this. Will you forgive me, Donald?"

What if Heidi pulled Melania aside and told her she would be by her side during the grueling months ahead and understood what the pressure feels like? She might even have helped her with her speech and spared her the embarrassment of an inexperienced aid typing out comments from an earlier speech given by first lady Michelle Obama!

Can you not see the Trumps being powerfully impacted? This very well may have been the first exposure they've ever had to authentic Christianity lived out in the real world.

Now, imagine Senator Cruz watching Donald and Melania's response and being convinced that there was a sincere regret in Donald for what both their wives had gone through. What if the senator, at this time, added that he would be honored to endorse Donald at the upcoming convention? It would not require much imagination to see Senator Cruz become the most influential spiritual and political voice in the Trump family. And if his influence helped Trump get elected, his proximity to power would serve him, Trump, and the nation.

This is the price we pay when we talk Christian but act like mere men when the rubber meets the road.

Honoring His Commitment

It wasn't until 46 days before the presidential election that Senator Cruz wrote in a Facebook post announcing his decision to endorse the Republican nominee, "If you don't want to see a Hillary Clinton presidency, I encourage you to vote for him."

Senator Cruz went on to list six policy reasons for why he was backing Trump, beginning with the importance of appointing conservatives to the Supreme Court. Other reasons for the about-face included "Obamacare"—which Trump has vowed to repeal the day he enters office—national security, immigration, and Trump's newfound support for Cruz's push against the Obama administration to move to relinquish U.S. oversight of an internet master directory of web addresses.[6]

Deliberate Saboteurs?

The Republican Party has given a lot to former President George W. Bush, Governor Mitt Romney, Senator Ted Cruz and Governor John Kasich. These men owe something back. At a minimum, they should not be saboteurs to Trump and Governor Pence.

Governor Kasich is popular in Ohio. He knows that Ohio is the quintessential "swing state," meaning its outcome moves the entire election in one direction or the other. Denying success in Ohio is the ultimate weapon of revenge.

In every election since 1960, the candidate who won Ohio won the presidency! It's a state where Republicans have been relatively competitive during the Obama era, losing by five points in 2008 and three points in 2012.

Did you know that a New York Times article reports Trump reached out to Governor Kasich through his son to discuss a possible role as vice president?[7] Some sort of conversation took place, but Kasich wasn't interested. Trump's team later denied such an offer was made. The fact is, Governor Kasich also has a personal issue with Trump. He is supporting other down ticket candidates up for re-election but not honoring the pledge he gave to support the Republican nominee.

Speaking a day after the Republican Convention, he said, "My position is, I'd like to see Donald become a unifier and positive. We just have some fundamental disagreements,"[8] he said, chuckling, "including a few areas: trade, immigration, foreign policy."[8]

The truth is, Trump reached out to Governor Kasich to help him unify the party, but the Governor didn't have the will to respond. In my opinion, if Governor Kasich doesn't come out like Senator Cruz and support Trump, and Trump loses Ohio, then the election loss will be caused by him. I'm believing Kasich will turn around.

On the other hand, the Left never seems to break rank. Trump can survive some of these hits, but in a close election the cumulative weight of all the National Reviews and Glen Becks and Mitt Romneys cannot help.

A Call To Love

Considering that we are called to love our enemies, even Trump qualifies for forgiveness. But when you consider that Trump is himself not an evangelical, but one who aspires to be a good Christian nonetheless, a Senator Cruz moment or Governor Kasich reconciliation could have had incredible power as a learning experience for Trump. It could have had a solidifying impact on both the kingdom and a political movement.

Have you ever seen the last formal portrait of Abraham Lincoln? Taken by Alexander Gardner, December 31, 1864, it is a stark contrast with the image of Lincoln as he began his term in office. His care worn features deeply fixed, he gazes out with an expression resembling a weary but contented sage. Lincoln came to office with little support from the revival preachers of his day because he did not openly attend any church. Yet his ordeal in office drove him to seek God, read the Bible and seek guidance in the national crisis. In doing so, his second inaugural address reads like a sermon. He was reshaped from self-reliant to God-dependent through the ordeal of the second American crucible. Trump, if elected, will likewise be shaped by pressures coming upon the Oval Office from the American unraveling and reset. What if God is reshaping Donald Trump on the potter's wheel from a strong-willed, self-made man to a humbler yet enduring prophetic prototype for America?

> LINCOLN WAS RESHAPED FROM SELF-RELIANT TO GOD-DEPENDANT

His bond with evangelicals is quite real and, as already quoted, he does not know that he deserves the devotion of evangelicals. Can you realistically think Hillary Clinton is being shaped by spiritual encounters in the same way? Do you see her being changed in the future?

Secretary Clinton, like President Obama, is an ideologue. Remember that. They have a fixed way of seeing the world. They have friends and enemies. That's their worldview. Your concerns are, in their minds, the concerns of their opponents. To Trump, there is no ideology, just issue-by-issue decisions.

This might be the appropriate place to say that I don't agree with all Trump's positions on social issues. But even on these matters the reason we are losing ground at such a rapid pace in our society is that, to those around us, what defines us is our political stances, not love, joy and peace.

An apologist friend, Dr. Michael Brown, recently shared that it is of paramount importance that he be able to fully step into the shoes of the person he is debating. Empathy is needed. This is how he engages the gay community and how he has formed a bond with African Americans when he agrees or disagrees with them on a broadcast.

If we want to establish a Christian witness, we need to concentrate more on who *we are* as we defend our ideas and cast our votes. If our witness is only political, we lose.

Endnotes

1. Retrieved from http://www.dailywire.com/news/7665/exclusive-cruz-camp-trump-campaign-approved-speech-ben-shapiro

2. MSNBC, *The Place for Politics 2016*, 7/20/16 Retrieved from http://mediamatters.org/embed/static/clips/2016/07/20/47907/msnbc-rnc-2016720-matthewscruzbadbehavior.

3. Retrieved from http://time.com/4416407/republican-convention-newt-gingrich-ted-cruz-transcript-video-speech/.

4. Retrieved from http://www.politico.com/story/2016/07/newt-gingrich-ted-cruz-225936.

5. Retrieved from http://time.com/4416845/ted-cruz-wont-vote-hillary-clinton/.

6. Retrieved from http://www.theatlantic.com/politics/archive/2016/09/cruz-endorsement-trump/501485/.

7. Retrieved from http://www.nytimes.com/2016/07/20/magazine/how-donald-trump-picked-his-running-mate.html?_r=0.

8. Retrieved from http://articles.philly.com/2016-07-24/news/74661974_1_donald-trump-john-kasich-trump-campaign.

9. Retrieved from http://articles.philly.com/2016-07-24/news/74661974_1_donald-trump-john-kasich-trump-campaign.

CHAPTER 8

"LEAD US NOT INTO TRUMPTATION ..."

As a proponent of Donald Trump, the "anointed Cyrus" that I believe is the ideal "chaos candidate" to guide us through the storm of the American unraveling, I have run into strong reactions ... some of them quite shocking.

It usually works like this: I'm having a polite conversation with a friend in a restaurant or perhaps I strike up a conversation with a stranger sitting next to me on a long flight. I normally try to avoid these types of scenarios on long flights; however, once in a while, if I come across a person that seems especially interesting, I will put down my book or computer and engage. Recently I was sitting next to an inexperienced flier who lived in Boston. She was a professional who worked in the mental health field for 30 years. The moment I helped her figure out how to open her tray and adjust her seat, I knew I was in trouble. She wanted to talk.

We discussed various schools of psychology from Rogers to Ellis and the conversation was laughingly cordial up to the moment she asked me why I was flying out of New York. I quietly mentioned having an appointment at Trump Towers, at which point I noted a pattern I had seen before. The very mention of Trump—even if related to a building—evokes the first wave of a neurological breakdown. Trump haters cannot resist making a comment, usually a mock shudder with the phrase, "Oooh, I can't stand that man." This has happened more than once. The silence on my end only heightens the tension. They look up quizzically as if waiting for the return secret handshake. I usually ask, "Have you ever met Mr. Trump?" They never answer that question. Instead they move directly into stage two on the Trump delirium index. They yell out "WHAT? Don't tell me you support him!" This exclamation is loud enough to disrupt the business class cabin, or, as I've experienced, an entire restaurant. It is also accompanied by a physical move away from me either in leaning back on the chair or shuffling the seat away, as if I am a Zika-infected mosquito and might be contagious.

Trump Delirium Index

What makes this curious to me is the literal distress seen on their faces. As the lady on the airplane put it, "Up until now I thought you were a nice person ... an intelligent man ... I actually liked you!" At this point the conversation shifts, depending on how and where they are located on the Trump Delirium Index.

There are three levels of belief on any subject. The higher up you go, the more emotionally and mentally committed you are to your idea. This works for good ideas and bad ideas:

- **Level 1—Opinion:** This is usually based on media information sources, social media interaction and peer group social trends.

- **Level 2—Belief:** This represents a stronger version of opinions based on certain assumptions of truth.

- **Level 3—Conviction:** This is a core belief that has strong feelings and arguments attached to it. At Level 3, a person's identity is wrapped up in their belief.

The scariest aspect to sustaining a functional democracy is the assumption of an educated and informed public. Most people are low information voters. They don't really examine their beliefs—they sort of pick them up by accident.

This is what makes liberal bias in media one of the greatest threats to democracy. Liberal media combined with peer pressure usually wins the battle for youth. Most people, especially youth, want to be liked and part of the "in" crowd. Ronald Reagan made it socially acceptable to be a conservative and Donald Trump made it socially acceptable to have opinions that do not line up with liberal dogma. That is the gift of the "wrecking ball."

The truth is, many liberals are a hoot to hang out with ... until you get to certain subjects. Most of the ones I've talked to do not know any informed or likable evangelicals or social conservatives. Frankly, I'd rather have a beer and conversation with a fellow Bucks County journalist like Chris Matthews of MSNBC then hide my beer from a disapproving Christian. The truth is, most educated liberals have stereotypes about conservative Christians that are never challenged by personal interaction. At this point in history, missionaries may be more needed in the media and Manhattan than Mozambique.

The average American who doesn't like Trump is usually responding to the stereotype of him that has been sketched out by the media. They are operating at Level 1/Opinion or Level 2/Belief.

Understand the "30 Second Law"

Speaking boldly on behalf of the truth is especially challenging for Christian conservatives because the Left is extremely adept at labeling and demonizing their opposition.

> THE LEFT IS EXTREMELY ADEPT AT LABELING AND DEMONIZING THEIR OPPOSITION

Most people do not realize that they form a first impression within 30 seconds or less. We all do it. The brain works almost like an old-fashioned camera. The moment we meet someone we begin taking a picture and sorting out whether we like or don't like them, if we agree or disagree with the image in front of us. We form a snapshot. The insidious truth is that one wrong first impression requires 30 new impressions to undo the imprint of our initial image.

The Shout Heard Around the World

In the political process the "30 Second Law" is on steroids. Type "Howard Dean" into Google search and the second item that comes up in the autocomplete search predictions list is "Howard Dean Yell." The incident happened on the night of the Iowa Democratic Caucus, January 19, 2004. It quickly became known as "the Scream," and it is a textbook study of how a brief gaffe, if given saturation coverage by the media, can brand and damage a politician's image for life.

That evening, Dean appeared before a crowd of downcast supporters in West Des Moines. He took off his suit jacket, rolled up the sleeves of his blue shirt, and acknowledged, "I'm sure there are some disappointed people here." Then he tried to motivate them to continue the fight. Getting revved up by the crowd's cheers and chants, he promised to take his campaign on to New Hampshire, South Carolina, California, and a string of other states, the names of which he shouted out like a cheerleader at a high school pep rally. His face reddening and his right hand balled into a fist, Dean shouted: "And then we're going to Washington, D.C.—to take back the White House—YEEEEEAAARGH!"[1]

The moment of exhortation was described in the media as the "primal scream" or the "'I Have a Scream Speech." It was replayed endlessly on national TV and immediately became the target of ridicule by the late-night talk show hostss, adding to Dean's embarrassment.

"Did you see Dean's speech last night?" asked Jay Leno. "Oh my God! Now I hear the cows in Iowa are afraid of getting mad Dean disease. It's always a bad sign when at the end of your speech, your aide is shooting you with a tranquilizer gun."

David Letterman joked: "Here's what happened: The people of Iowa realized they didn't want a president with the personality of a hockey dad." It all made Dean, normally a very disciplined and straitlaced New Englander, look more than a little bit "kooky." That moment ended his legitimacy as a Democratic candidate.[2]

Al Gore wanted to score points with voters by saying he would put Medicare and Social Security in a "lock box," but he made the mistake of repeating the term too often in a debate with George Bush. Saturday Night Live took hold of that moment in a debate reenactment and rebranded Gore's identity, turning him into a nerdy techno geek. In comparison, the spoof done on George W. Bush making up the word "strategery" made him less pretentious. In the end, George won by a hanging chad and Gore lost his presidency in a lockbox.

The Surprise Gaffe

The greatest gaffe so far in the presidential election has not come from political novice Trump, but from a far more experienced politician.

It's one thing to label your opponent, but it's another thing to label everyone voting for them. As a rule, you never attack your opponent's supporters. Theoretically, at some point a winner in the presidential contest will have to present themselves as a leader for all people. That is hard to do if you attack the half that voted for "the other guy." This is why the following blunder is hard to understand as it slanders with a broad brush half the Republican electorate.

During a fundraiser in New York City on Friday, September 9, 2016, Hillary Clinton described Americans supporting Donald Trump as a "basket of deplorables" made up of "racist, sexist, homophobic, xenophobic, Islamophobic"[3] people.

The exact quote is: "You know to just be grossly generalistic, you could put half of Trump's supporters into what I call the basket of deplorables,"[4] she said as the crowd laughed and applauded. "... The racist, sexist, homophobic, xenophobic, Islamophobic, you name it."[5]

Clinton said it was unfortunate that Trump had given them a voice, citing "offensive mean-spirited rhetoric" on websites and Twitter.

"Some of those folks—they are irredeemable, but thankfully they are not America," she said.

In comparison, she praised the supporters attending her fundraiser as "friends" who were in the "other basket." Following Clinton's comments, Barbra Streisand performed a parody of the song "Send in the Clowns,"[6] which mocked Trump.

What makes this quote most troubling is that it was not a comment made by accident, it was a scripted statement read on purpose. Statements like that are calculated to energize the base. This quote was a huge miscalculation, however, because it exposed what liberals really think about Americans and, in so doing, revealed the elitism and disconnect between liberal ideology and the rest of the nation.

Not surprisingly, the greatest gaffe received minimal news mention.

Pōtātō, Pōtătō

Vice President Dan Quayle experienced this moment in Trenton on June 15, 1992—and this was before the Internet. It was the day Quayle did a media stop at Trenton's Munoz Rivera School that a simple spelling bee ended his career. He misspelled potato as "potatoe."

In his 1994 memoir, Quayle devotes a whole chapter to the incident in a classroom and the impact it had on his career.

"It was a defining moment of the worst kind imaginable,"[7] Quayle wrote in the autobiography. "Politicians live and die by the symbolic sound byte."[8]

Less than five months after the incident, both Quayle and President Bush were voted out of office, replaced by President Bill Clinton and Vice President Al Gore.

A few days after the spelling mishap, Quayle sat down with a group of top American reporters for a televised two-hour discussion of important issues. He was seeking to stifle the media assault that he was intellectually challenged. The newsmen, and viewers, were left with the impression that for all the jokes about him, the vice president was actually very bright and well-informed. Quayle was in fact a politically savvy and smart young man, but from then on, the potato incident became a campaign weapon for Democrats backing Clinton and Gore.

On Sept 11, 2008, Sarah Palin did an interview in which she referenced the proximity of Russia to an Alaskan island.[9] Two days later, on the 2008 season premiere of *Saturday Night Live*, Tina Fey appeared in a sketch portraying Sarah Palin, and spoofed Governor Palin's remark.[10] Palin never said the line Fey delivered, but the image played into the media's narrative against Palin nonetheless. When the media is out to get you, they simply make stuff up.

Into this study of dangerous sound bites and unforgiving consequences steps a sheer rhetorical anomaly—Donald Trump. Nobody can figure out how he survives. He is the political equivalent of Neo dodging bullets in the *The Matrix*.

What Did Trump Actually Say ... About Mexicans?

There is no quote as distorted as the "all Mexicans are rapists" sound bite manipulated by Democrats to block the Latino vote.

For an interesting perspective on this, I encourage you to read a thoughtful article in Salon Magazine written by Alberto A. Martinez, a Puerto Rican professor and Bernie Sanders supporter.

Martinez writes:

> The media needs to stop telling this lie about Donald Trump. I'm a Sanders supporter—and value honesty. Trump's words on Mexicans have been misconstrued by all sides. This liberal, Puerto Rican professor says enough!
>
> In one of my courses, at the University of Texas at Austin, I asked my students: "What has Donald Trump said that you found most offensive?" One student raised her hand high: "He said that all Mexicans are rapists." I asked a coworker the same question. He replied: "He said that all Mexican immigrants are rapists."
>
> I explained that Trump said no such thing. This is what Trump said:
>
>> "When do we beat Mexico at the border? They're laughing at us, at our stupidity ... When Mexico sends its people they're not sending their best. They're

not sending you; they're not sending you. They're sending people that have lots of problems, and they're bringing those problems with us. They're bringing drugs. They're bringing crime. They're rapists, and some, I assume, are good people. But I speak to border guards and they tell us what we're getting."

You might well dislike Trump's words. I did. But let's not make it worse. He did not say that all Mexicans are rapists. Yet that's what many commentators did. For example, Politico misquoted Trump by omitting his phrase about "good people." They said he was "demonizing Mexicans as rapists." They argued that Mexicans do not really commit more rapes in the U.S. than whites. But that's not what Trump claimed.

Similarly, other news sources misrepresented his words in offensive ways:

- *The New York Times:* "Trump's claim that illegal Mexican immigrants are 'rapists.'"

- *Time Magazine:* "Trump's comment that Mexican immigrants are 'rapists.'"

- *Associated Press:* "Trump called Mexican immigrants rapists and criminals"CBS News: "Trump defends calling Mexican immigrants 'rapists.'"

- *L.A. Times:* "describing Mexican immigrants as 'rapists.'"

- *Fortune:* "in a speech branding Mexican immigrants as criminals and rapists."Hollywood Reporter: "he referred to Mexican immigrants as 'rapists.'"

- *Huffington Post:* "He called Latino immigrants 'criminals' and 'rapists.'"

- *The Washington Post:* "He referred to Mexicans as 'rapists.'"

Compare such words with Trump's words. Which is worse? Writers excerpted the phrase: "they're rapists," as if it were about all Mexican unauthorized immigrants, or worse, about all Mexican immigrants, or even worst, about all Mexicans. But that's not what he said. That's not what he meant. It was just a remark about some of the criminals crossing the border.

The trick for misrepresenting Trump's words can be used against anyone.

Professor Martinez went on to use Hillary Clinton's quote as an example from the October 17, 2015, Democratic debate: "When asked 'Which enemy are you most proud of?' Hillary replied: 'In addition to the NRA, um, the health insurance companies, the drug companies, um, the Iranians.'"[11]

If Trump had made this statement the *New York Times* and CNN would be bleating and Tweeting that Donald Trump says he is "proud to be the enemy of 77 million citizens of Iran, plus millions more living outside Iran, including mothers, children, and disabled people"![12]

"Did [Mr. Trump] unfairly single out Mexicans when complaining about crimes by unauthorized immigrants?"[13]

Here are the facts. Mexico is the leading source of illegal immigration coming into the U.S. "[R]oughly 76 percent of criminal unauthorized immigrants[14] are from Mexico."[15]

What Kind of Criminal Activity are We Talking About?

According to Martinez, "The Texas Department of Public Safety identified 207,076[16] foreign aliens who were booked into Texas county jails from October 2008 through August 1, 2014. Their term 'foreign aliens' includes both foreigners who are in Texas legally and foreigners who entered illegally." This company of 207,076 aliens was "accused of 357,884 crimes in those 70 months." They were charged with "4,413 terroristic threats, 60,973 robberies and larcenies, 6,636 vehicle thefts, 78,682 assaults, 12,869 sexual assaults and offenses, 1,113 kidnappings, and 3,089 homicides."[17]

The number of sexual assaults per year, in Texas alone, averages 1,383 incidents reported and if including incidents not reported, the number is closer to 4000 rapes and sexual assaults according to the National Crime and Victimization Survey, 2008-2012.[18]

HOW MUCH CRIME IS CAUSED BY LEAVING OUR NATION'S DOOR UNLOCKED?

"In Texas, roughly 529 foreigners per year were accused of committing murder. Plus, the FBI reports that 36 percent of homicides nationwide remain unsolved."[19]

We lock our doors at night. How many of these homicides are caused by leaving the nation's door unlocked?

Putting All This in Perspective

These crime rates are staggering and should jolt you awake.

Martinez references the football stadium at the University of Texas at Austin to grasp the scope of this issue.[20] But I live near Dallas, Texas, where the Cowboys play football, so I'd like to bring the example a little closer to home. The Cowboy's home games are played at the AT&T Stadium. This massive structure seats 80,000 but with standing room included it can hold over 100,000 fans. In fact, this stadium holds the record for attendance at an NFL game. It happened in 2009 when a crowd of 105,121 fans packed the stadium wall to wall.[21]

There is nothing that compares to the full throated roar of 100,000 people packed into a stadium.

Remember that 207,076 aliens were accused of 357,884 crimes in 70 months. If we gathered all those illegals together in one place we would have enough criminal aliens to fill two AT&T Stadiums and enough crime committed to pack 3 and 1/2 AT&T Stadiums with suffering victims.

Before you understand the magnitude of the numbers, it is easy to misread what Trump is trying to say. Each murder touched a whole family. A wife who lost her husband. Parents who never saw their child again. This is real human suffering. Each sexual assault cuts into a human life. Not one of the men or women killed or assaulted in Texas by unauthorized immigrants would have been touched if Washington took seriously the need to keep the wrong people from entering the U.S. illegally.

I'm sure you get the point. Weak borders are an invitation to drugs, murders, rapes and gangs. What about terrorists? According to data from the Department of Homeland Security (DHS), if elected president, Hillary Clinton could permanently resettle 500,000 to 800,000 or as many as 1 million Muslim migrants during the first term of her presidency alone.[22]

What does all of this mean for the future of the United States? Author Mark Steyn put it clearly in an interview with Bill O'Reilly, saying, "there is a crude arithmetic here, Bill which is that the more Muslims you have, the more terrorism you have. So, that France, Belgium and Germany have very high Muslim populations, and they have a lot of terrorism. When you were in Poland and the Czech Republic, they have very few Muslims so they don't have terrorism."[23] 1 million more Muslims equals more terrorism. Crude but simple arithmetic.

As I've said, Trump's wall is a physical symbol of a spiritual reality —*"Like a city that is broken into and without walls Is a man who has no control over his spirit"* (Proverbs 25:28). America needs Cyrus and an army of Nehemiahs to restore the walls.

Let's take a look at the rest of Trump's supposedly outrageous quote about Mexicans:

And it only makes common sense, it only makes common sense: they're sending us not the right people, and it's coming from more than Mexico, it's coming from all over South and Latin America, and it's coming probably, probably from the Middle East. But we don't know because we have no protection, and we have no competence. We don't know what's happening. And it's gotta stop. And it's gotta stop fast.[24]

Makes sense. Yes?

What Does Hillary Clinton Believe About All This?

Hillary and the Democrats want open borders, amnesty for the 11 million illegal aliens already living here and an increase in immigration quotas in general. They like open borders. Do you know why? It isn't about being humanitarian or having compassion. It's about power. They want the votes and the data suggests that immigrants will give them those votes.[25] They know that if they promise free benefits and entitlements, they will get millions of new voters. Are they willing to do this at the risk of bankrupting the nation? Yes. There will always be an economist to tell them that though the nation is in 19 trillion dollars of debt and immigration will add 6 trillion more to the debt, the numbers will work out later.

The most cynical among them know this will lead to a collapse, but they also know they will always have a job. They understand that if the nation is bankrupt, they will be, in the end, the only party in power. This is how closet Marxist revolutionaries think and this is why Hillary's plan is dangerous. Her policies fall in line with key members of the shadow cabinet who are intent on remaking America.

What about Republicans? Why are they silent? They are for amnesty, but for different reasons. Their donors want access to all that cheap labor! Republicans also see the rising number of Hispanic voters and want to avoid looking bad. They think Hispanics will love them and be more supportive if they embrace amnesty.

And of course there is another side to consider. What about those solid, hard-working, contributing illegals? A pastor friend of mine told me he has a second church service made up of these beautiful families. The thought of their church and individual families being torn apart by forced deportation is heart breaking. This seems to be the place where policy needs to be flexible. But what about securing the border for the future and protecting citizens from those that are among us who are likely to commit crimes?

Hillary's position will shock you. She believes the border is secure enough, saying during a CNN Univision debate: "We have the most secure border we've ever had ..." She wants to give citizenship to all illegal aliens, which would give them access to welfare, voting privileges, and the ability to bring over their absent family members through migration.[26] How much will this cost? Her full amnesty for illegal immigrants will cost U.S. taxpayers $6.3 trillion, according to a report from the Heritage Foundation.[27] Clinton's proposal is that illegal entry is not in and of itself a deportable offense. Therefore, if you can get in you can stay in. Millions of people will be able to illegally come to the country and, once here, they can apply for federal benefits, attend U.S. schools, receive affirmative action, take jobs, and give birth to children who receive birthright citizenship.

Under Clinton's plan, when will a potential illegal alien be deported? After a violent crime and conviction has been obtained! "Deportation laws will be enforced *after* an American is victimized, raped, or murdered by a criminal alien. The new federal policy will wait to enforce immigration laws after there is a criminal conviction. This means we will be admitting and releasing criminals by the hundreds of thousands, (Stadiums full) and letting them roam free until after they have committed a crime, been apprehended, tried, and convicted for that crime.[28] As Senator Sessions of Alabama has explained, immigration laws ought to remove criminal aliens *before* they are convicted of a violent crime. "There is no delicate balancing act here, we need to remove potentially violent offenders before they hurt innocent families—before the irreversible occurs"[29]

What Did Trump Actually Say ... About Muslims?

One day after the June 19, mass shooting at the Orlando nightclub Pulse that killed 49 people, Donald Trump said if he were President, he would use his executive power to put in place an immigration hold on Muslims and some people from Middle Eastern countries. His concern is that refugees could be America's "Trojan horse." Trump told a crowd at St. Anselm College in New Hampshire Monday afternoon, "This could be a better, bigger more horrible version than the legendary Trojan horse ever was."[30]

He continued, "Altogether, under the Clinton plan, you'd be admitting hundreds of thousands of refugees from the Middle East with no system to vet them, or to prevent the radicalization of their children." Trump said he wants a "common-sense" immigration policy that "promotes American values."

"The immigration laws of the United States give the president powers to suspend entry into the country of any class of persons," Trump said. "Now, any class, it really is determined and to be determined by the president. For the interests of the United States. And it's as he or she deems appropriate."

"I will use this power to protect the American people," he continued. "When I'm elected I will suspend immigration from areas of the world where there is a proven history of terrorism against the United States, Europe or our allies, until we fully understand how to end these threats."

Though the Orlando shooter Omar Mateen was an American citizen, Trump suggested immigrants from the Middle East can come to the U.S. and radicalize people who are already here, or work to convince them online.

"The media talks about homegrown terrorism," Trump said. "But Islamic radicalism … and the networks that nurture it are imports from overseas whether you like it or don't like it."[31]

Trump said the ban would be lifted "when as a nation we're in a position to properly and perfectly screen these people coming into our country."

Trump went on to challenge Hillary Clinton for saying the U.S. should allow Syrian refugees. "If drastic action isn't taken," Trump said, there will be "nothing left of the United States. If we don't get tough, and if we don't get smart—and fast—we're not going to have our country anymore," he said. "There will be nothing, absolutely nothing left."

In an interview with Greta Van Susteren of Fox News, Trump discussed a committee he was organizing to study immigration issues and the proposed Muslim ban. At one point, Van Susteren asked Trump: "Have you decided whether you will back off on the ban?"

"Sure, I would back off on it —I would like to back off as soon as possible because, frankly, I would like to see something happen, but we have to be vigilant," Trump responded. "There is a radical Islamic terrorism problem that, you know, our president doesn't want to talk about. All you have to do is take a look at the World Trade Center, take a look at San Bernardino or Paris, what a disaster that was, and so many other locations ... We're going to have to solve the problem."

Van Susteren pressed Trump, wanting to know if American Muslims would be banned. Trump said all Americans would be allowed in and that there would only be exceptions for some foreigners. He made clear that this would be a temporary ban and said, "Ultimately, it's my aim to have it lifted."

"Right now there is no ban, but I would like to see—there has to be an idea, there has to be something, because there are some pretty bad things going on," Trump said. "And I have Muslim friends, great Muslim friends who are telling me: 'You are so right. There is something going on that we have to get to the bottom of it.' So we will see what happens."

For Trump, the issue was never about targeting a particular religion. It was about protecting Americans by applying a common sense solution.

FOR TRUMP THE ISSUE WAS NEVER ABOUT TARGETING A SPECIFIC RELIGION, BUT PROTECTING AMERICANS

What Did Trump Actually Say ... About Saddam?

At a July 2016 campaign rally in North Carolina, Trump made a controversial comment about Saddam Hussein, saying, "He was a bad guy—really bad guy. But you know what? He did well. He killed terrorists. He did that so well. They didn't read them their rights. They didn't talk. They were terrorists. Over. Today, Iraq is Harvard for terrorism." *The New York Times,*[32] *Washington Post*[33] and CNN[34] and other liberal media hit squads all led with the same words "Donald Trump Praises Saddam Hussein," and added some variation of these words "for Being Good at killing Terrorists."

Trump's comments about Saddam Hussein were accurate, in so far as they address his handling of Islamic radicalism in Iraq.

Clare Lopez, vice president for research and analysis for the Center for Security Policy, accused America's leaders of failing to recognize Islam for what it is:

> Our top leadership has never understood what Islam really is and implemented policies they thought were going to empower "democratic forces" against dictators—never realizing the reason those dictators were able to hold things together was precisely because they suppressed jihad, and that if they let up the pressure or if genuinely free elections were held, the jihadist would win—or at least surge back up to cause mayhem again.[35]

Americans think of religion as one thing and politics as another. We will not understand radical Islam until we understand that many Muslims view their faith as both a political movement and a religious ideology. The appeal of ISIS is the vision that a geographic caliphate can be formed where the religious and political merger of Islam can be made manifest in great power and glory as it once was in the Middle East. Think of Islam as a political ideology wrapped in the shell of a religion and you see why moderates have a hard time inspiring the grass roots.

Donald Trump is more aware of this challenge than are the Democrats or beltway Republicans.

Trump's comments on Saddam, Muslims and Mexicans make sense if you hear them without the spin of the all-pervasive Left in media.

When The Wrecking Ball Started Rolling

What is it about this man, Donald Trump, that frightens globalists, liberals, media, academia and the ruling establishment class in politics?

Trump is a threat to the "Ruling Class," a term used by Angelo Codevilla to describe a relatively small number of elites whose thought processes, goals and philosophies are very much different than the nation at large.

Codevilla says that, "Today's ruling class, from Boston to San Diego, was formed by an educational system that exposed them to the same ideas and gave them remarkably uniform guidance, as well

! habits. These amount to a social canon of judgments ͜ and evil, complete with secular sacred history, sins (against minorities and the environment), and saints."[36] Only a small percentage of Americans agree with the thought process, philosophies, goals and objectives of the ruling class. in the country class, and we do not believe that government is God.

Codevilla explains, "What really distinguishes these privileged people demographically is that, whether in government power directly or as officers in companies, their careers and fortunes depend on government."

It seems that Democrats and Republicans have performed a Vulcan mind-meld and become elites that have more in common with each other than the people they represent. The values of the "fly over" Red State country have not changed. They still have a genuine commitment to smaller government, fiscal discipline, family and religious liberty, but these issues are no longer the passion of establishment Republicans.

ESTABLISHMENT REPUBLICANS AND DEMOCRATS ARE UNDER THE SPELL OF THE SAME SPIRIT

The common ground between Sanders' and Trump's populist following is a frustration with the Ruling Class. As the election nears, news of Bush family members supporting Hillary is a testament to the fact that there really is not much difference between establishment Republicans and Democrats after all. They are under the spell of the same spirit.

The Clintons and their political machine are so much a part of this establishment group that the Romneys, Bushes and other Ruling

Class politicians would rather see Trump defeated and a progressive in the White House then trust an outsider coming to power. Trump is invading the gentleman's club and breaking something up.

Endnotes

1. http://www.usnews.com/news/articles/2008/01/17/the-battle-cry-that-backfired.
2. Ibid.
3. http://www.breitbart.com/2016-presidential-race/2016/09/09/hillary-clintons-47-percent-moment-calls-trump-supporters-racist-sexist-homophobic-xenophobic-islamaphobic/.
4. http://www.politifact.com/truth-o-meter/article/2016/sep/11/context-hillary-clinton-basket-deplorables/.
5. Ibid.
6. https://www.youtube.com/watch?v=aHhjwtMBSN4.
7. http://www.capitalcentury.com/1992.html.
8. http://www.foxnews.com/politics/2014/03/07/obama-flubs-spelling-respect.html.
9. https://www.youtube.com/watch?v=iGSJCDw3ZBw.
10. http://www.nbc.com/saturday-night-live/video/sarah-palin-and-hillary-clinton-address-the-nation/n12287 (1:36).
11. http://www.salon.com/2015/12/21/the_media_needs_to_stop_telling_this_lie_about_donald_trump_im_a_sanders_supporter_and_value_honesty/.
12. Ibid.
13. Ibid.
14. Ibid.
15. https://www.dhs.gov/sites/default/files/publications/table41d.xls.
16. http://www.salon.com/2015/12/21/the_media_needs_to_stop_telling_this_lie_about_donald_trump_im_a_sanders_supporter_and_value_honesty/.
17. https://minutemanproject.com/3089-homicides-by-illegal-immigrants-since-2008-in-texas/.
18. http://www.salon.com/2015/12/21/the_media_needs_to_stop_telling_this_lie_about_donald_trump_im_a_sanders_supporter_and_value_honesty/.
19. Ibid.
20. Ibid.
21. http://www.nfl.com/news/story/09000d5d812c91b4/article/nfl-regularseasonrecord-crowd-of-105121-sees-giantscowboys.

22.	http://www.breitbart.com/2016-presidential-race/2016/07/14/clinton-resettle-one-million-muslim-migrants-first-term-alone/.

23.	http://www.steynonline.com/7553/the-left-would-rather-ban-the-debate-than-win-it.

24.	http://www.salon.com/2015/12/21/the_media_needs_to_stop_telling_this_lie_about_donald_trump_im_a_sanders_supporter_and_value_honesty/.

25.	http://www.pewresearch.org/fact-tank/2013/07/22/are-unauthorized-immigrants-overwhelmingly-democrats/.

26.	http://www.breitbart.com/2016-presidential-race/2016/05/25/clinton-releases-plan-dissolve-us-border-within-100-days/.

27.	http://www.heritage.org/research/reports/2013/05/the-fiscal-cost-of-unlawful-immigrants-and-amnesty-to-the-us-taxpayer.

28.	http://www.breitbart.com/2016-presidential-race/2016/05/25/clinton-releases-plan-dissolve-us-border-within-100-days/.

29.	http://yellowhammernews.com/politics-2/sessions-introduces-legislation-to-end-sanctuary-cities-prevent-illegal-aliens-from-reentering-the-country/.

30.	http://www.cnn.com/TRANSCRIPTS/1606/13/cnr.06.html.

31.	https://www.youtube.com/watch?v=zV40c4bPCrA.

32.	http://www.nytimes.com/2016/07/06/us/politics/donald-trump-saddam-hussein.html.

33.	https://www.washingtonpost.com/news/post-politics/wp/2016/07/05/donald-trump-praises-saddam-hussein-for-killing-terrorists-so-good/.

34.	http://www.cnn.com/2016/07/05/politics/donald-trump-saddam-hussein-iraq-terrorism/.

35.	http://www.christiantoday.com/article/christian.thinkers.accuse.politicians.media.of.failing.to.name.islam.as.the.real.enemy.behind.terror.attacks/71974.htm.

36.	http://spectator.org/39326_americas-ruling-class-and-perils-revolution/.

CHAPTER 9

THE GREAT AMERICAN UNRAVELING

Make no mistake, what is happening to America right now (which we have covered briefly) is going to impact the world. Let's take a closer look at this subject covered briefly in chapter one.

A crucible is a container in which metals are melted or subjected to very high temperatures. When the Apostle Peter spoke to the Roman Christians who were facing Nero's coming persecution, he said, *"Beloved, think it not strange concerning the fiery trial which is to test you, as though some strange thing happened unto you…"* (1 Peter 4:12). He uses the word "fiery," or *purosis* in the Greek, to describe a refiner's fire where metal is tested.

The fiery trial comes both to believers and nations. It can be brief or prolonged and it can produce something better or worse. The result of the refiner's fire, often depends on the metal being tested.

Webster's dictionary describes a crucible as:

- A place or occasion of severe test or challenge; "the crucible of combat."

- A place or situation that forces people to change or make difficult decisions.

- A place or situation in which different elements interact to produce something new.

Here is what I have discovered—there are three stages in the crucible:

- **Stage 1:** An "unraveling" that culminates in a crisis.

- **Stage 2:** A "conflict" of ideologies, often arms, to determine a victor in the power clash.

- **Stage 3:** A "reset" that establishes the new reality or the next status quo.

America has experienced three tests that defined it as a nation. We are now entering a fourth historic crucible. Within its wake all economies, democracies and every church or ministry enjoying any degree of liberty will be globally affected. This subject is of massive importance.

We Have Been Here Before

As Solomon said, *"There is nothing new under the sun"* (Ecclesiastes 1:9). The struggle we are in has happened before in history.

- **The first crucible** was the founding of our nation during the American Revolutionary War. From 1775-1783, we were facing an ideological clash inside the nation that pitted Patriots against Tories who were citizens of the Colonies sympathetic to Britain. Thomas Paine writes famously in the pamphlet series,

"The American Crisis" that, "These are the times that try men's souls."

- **The second crucible** was the Civil War from 1860-1865. The conflict was north against south. The ideological clash was over the rights of States to leave the Union. The root of this was economic and driven by the agrarian south and its dependence on slave labor. Abraham Lincoln recounts in the Gettysburg Address of the crisis we faced saying, "Now we are engaged in a great civil war, testing whether that nation, or any nation so conceived and so dedicated, can long endure."

Abraham Lincoln spoke more like a prophet to our day than most people think. In an address in Springfield, in 1838, Lincoln addressed the early unravelling that would later culminate in the Civil War. Speaking of incidents familiar to his audience he said, "The increasing disregard for law, which pervades the country and accounts of outrages committed by mobs, form the everyday news of the times … At what point then, is the approach of danger to be expected? I answer, if it ever reaches us, it must spring up amongst us. It cannot come from abroad. If destruction be our lot, we must ourselves be its author and finisher. As a nation of freemen, we must live through all time, or die by suicide."[1]

- **The third crucible** was the Great Depression and WWII. This was a test of our survival, but was different than the first, second and fourth in that it was brought upon us from the outside. The forces that we were competing with were global ideologies that pitted democracy against dictators and emperors.

So How Did We Get Here?

Simply go back 50 years ago to the 1960s where you had students opposing the symbols of American authority and government. They wanted nothing to do with it. They opposed the military on campus at Kent State University in Ohio. They protested the Vietnam War and the banks. They distrusted and protested everything that symbolized the institutions of democracy.

The progressive radicals of the 1960s graduated from campus radicals to university professors. For decades now progressive liberals have been shaping the political leanings of malleable young minds. This is a testament to the track record of success that liberal education has had.

FOR DECADES PROGRESSIVE LIBERALS HAVE BEEN SHAPING MALLEABLE YOUNG MINDS

One of the women who laid the groundwork for the emergence of Ronald Reagan was a former Democrat turned Republican named Midge Decter—a great conservative intellectual thinker. She put it perfectly when explaining the thought process of this generation. It speaks so aptly to this point and reveals how easily entire generations can be indoctrinated:

> It might sound a paradoxical thing to say—for surely never has a generation of children occupied more sheer hours of parental time—but the truth is that we neglected you. We allowed you a charade of trivial freedoms in order to avoid making those impositions on you that are in the end both the

training ground and proving ground for true independence. We pronounced you strong when you were still weak in order to avoid the struggles with you that would have fed your true strength. We proclaimed you sound when you were foolish in order to avoid taking part in the long, slow, slogging effort that is the only route to genuine maturity of mind and feeling. Thus, it was no small anomaly of your growing up that while you were the most indulged generation, you were also in many ways the most abandoned to your own meager devices by those into whose safe-keeping you had been given.

Today, 50 years later, students want to get further in bed with all of that. As it is in all cunningly devised uprisings, the dream of utopia is wrapped in words such as liberty, progress, happiness, reason and nature. They want to be taken care of by the government. There's no longer any suspicion. There's no longer any doubt. There's no longer any distrust. The government has gone from "Big Brother" to the father figure taking care of the family. We have now gone full circle in 50 years, from anti-American liberalism to Marxist Socialist communism.

The Soviets and Chinese communists are on the extreme left, and in the center you have the wonderful Democratic Party blending into moderates and independents.

What Can We Learn?

In the United States, where God and religion have been dethroned and where the goddess of reason has been enthroned, we find that democracy has become for us a system that elects officials who become the elite chosen to represent the masses.

When this "elite" group becomes too disconnected from the grassroots, they become like modern day monarchs—unresponsive to the nation as a whole. They begin to see the geography of red and blue states as a vast middle of America "flyover country"—the "red zone" as it's called.

Red zone Americans are hardworking, middle class voters. They are oftentimes Christian, and from old industrial towns that have been decimated by job losses, and are routinely stereotyped by this "ruling class of elites" as "backwards" or "ignorant."

President Obama in an unscripted moment while running for office said: "They (the red state Americans) get bitter, they cling to guns or religion or antipathy toward people who aren't like them or anti-immigrant sentiment or anti-trade sentiment as a way to explain their frustrations."[2]

It is the arrogance and disconnection of the "establishment" on the Left and Right that explains the populist uprising of Sanders and Trump disenfranchised youth and middle class.

As Hugh Hewitt says: "Donald Trump, like it or not—like him or not—is the imperfect messenger of the perfect storm in American politics. He is the shuddering, convulsive conclusion to decades of perceived indifference to the American middle class combined with a conviction that the GOP is spineless ..."[3]

Trump is the first candidate to seek office who owns no party agenda other than rescuing a system in danger of collapse by the spend-now-pay-later politically correct establishment who set it up. In the end, he is the only one with the "titanium will" to address the issues that will make a future for the next generation who will inherit the debt if the wrong person is in office during the "unraveling" and the fourth crucible.

In my meetings with Trump, and writing this account, I cannot help but wonder if the critics who attempt to liken him to Hitler, Mussolini or Stalin are not making the same mistake they made with Churchill. While Churchill is unmatched in terms of rhetorical skills, the similarities in personality, energy, leadership style, and prophetic intuition are unmistakable.

Winston Churchill's Warning

In light of secular, historical figures like Washington, Lincoln, Churchill and Thatcher, I believe Christians need to change their search criteria. We should start looking for evidence of who is anointed to get results rather than who is the most committed Christian. The battle for the survival of Christian civilization is already upon us. In regard to the threat against Christian civilization in the 1940s, we can hear the echo of Churchill speaking to us now.

At 5:30 a.m. on May 10, 1940, Nazi Germany began a massive attack against Holland, Belgium, Luxembourg, and France.

The German Blitzkrieg caught the Allies off guard. After just a few weeks of battle, Hitler's armies had conquered Holland, Luxembourg, and Belgium. Paris fell on June 14. Three days later, the French requested an armistice, or a truce.

The following day, June 18, British Prime Minister Winston Churchill spoke to the House of Commons. He addressed the disastrous turn of events in Europe, amid the stark realization that

Britain now stood alone against the seemingly unstoppable might of Hitler's military machine. He said the following:

> I expect that the Battle of Britain is about to begin. Upon this battle depends the survival of Christian civilization. Upon it depends our own British life, and the long continuity of our institutions and our Empire.
>
> ## UPON THIS BATTLE DEPENDS THE SURVIVAL OF CHRISTIAN CIVILIZATION
>
> The whole fury and might of the enemy must very soon be turned on us.
>
> Hitler knows that he will have to break us in this Island or lose the war. If we can stand up to him, all Europe may be free and the life of the world may move forward into broad, sunlit uplands. But if we fail, then the whole world, including the United States, including all that we have known and cared for, will sink into the abyss of a new Dark Age made more sinister, and perhaps more protracted, by the lights of perverted science.
>
> Let us therefore brace ourselves to our duties, and so bear ourselves that if the British Empire and its Commonwealth last for a thousand years, men will still say, "This was their finest hour."[4]

The question remains: What will Christians in America do? Will history record that this was our finest hour?

The Gravity of What We Are Dealing With

Presbyterian pastor and writer Francis A. Schaeffer stated: "The basic problem of the Christians in this country in the last eighty years or so, in regard to society and in regard to government, is that they have seen things in bits and pieces instead of totals. They have very gradually become disturbed over permissiveness, pornography, the public schools, the breakdown of the family, and finally abortion. But they have not seen this as a totality—each thing being a part, a symptom, of a much larger problem. They have failed to see that all of this has come about due to a shift in world view—that is, through a fundamental change in the overall way people think and view the world and life as a whole. This shift has been *away from* a worldview that was at least vaguely Christian in peoples memory (even if they were not individually Christian) *toward something completely different ...*"[5]

This is not a conflict as some would like to make it, between opposing political parties or economic views. It is a conflict of a much more fundamental and cosmic nature. In terms of our political and social unravelling, what we have before us in each day's news are the collision of these two incompatible views regarding ultimate moral authority.

Moral Authority

James Hunter writes: "The point needs to be made that all individuals ground their views of the world within some conception of moral authority. Not only those who are religious in a traditional sense, but also those who claim to have no religious faith at all base their views of the world in unprovable assumptions about 'being' and 'knowledge.'"[6]

The prevailing secular view embodied in the "progressive left" is that ultimate moral authority resides within the individual and their own definition of meaning and experience. According to this view, each individual is free to do what is right in his own eyes and no one, no external source, has the power to impose a definition on them. This expanded scope of self-definition is the reason why the letters have expanded to LGBT representing people redefining their very gender as transgender and transvestite.

Hunter says: "Within communities that hold orthodox views, moral authority arises from a common commitment to transcendence, by which I mean a dynamic reality that is independent of, prior to, and more powerful than human experience."

This is a point fundamental to the very existence of democratic self-governing people and should therefore be seriously considered as an indispensable aspect in the discipling of nations. How do we secure a culture of flourishing? The answer is rooted in how we define the basis of "moral authority." Is it in the individual or is it somewhere else?

The Founding Fathers of the United States—in varying degrees— understood very well the relationship between law and freedom and how one's worldview regarding this relates to government as they formed it to operate. One of the signers of the Declaration of Independence was a Presbyterian pastor and president of Princeton University named John Witherspoon (1723-1794). He served on various important committees related to the founding of the country.

Lex Rex

Schaeffer drives the point home saying, "John Witherspoon knew and stood consciously in the stream of Samuel Rutherford, a Scotsman who lived from 1600-1661, and who wrote *Lex Rex* in 1644. *Lex Rex* means LAW IS KING—a phrase that was absolutely earthshaking. In *Lex Rex* he wrote that the law, and no one else, is king. Therefore the heads of government are under the law, not a law unto themselves."[7]

The men who gathered to debate the new form of government they were creating in Philadelphia were profoundly learned. Jefferson was a deist who drew vastly from the well of John Locke who took *Lex Rex* and made a profound secular application of the ideas.

As Schaeffer says, "These men really knew what they were doing. We are not reading back into history what was not there. We cannot say too strongly that they really understood the basis of government, which they were founding. Think of the great flaming phrase "certain inalienable rights." Who gives these rights? The state? Then they were not inalienable because the state can change them and take them away. Where do these rights come from?"

The answer is clear in the documents they wrote. "We hold these truths to be self-evident, that all men are created equal, that they are endowed by their Creator with certain unalienable rights ..."

The Creator of man is the basis of these rights. They recognized that law could be king because there was a Law Giver, a Person to give these inalienable rights to mankind.

Most people do not know that from the beginning, prayer opened the national congress. These men knew that they were building an infrastructure on a foundation that referenced a Supreme Being and Creator as the foundation of a moral society. They knew that without this foundation everything they were building would be nonsense.

Now, everything that was fought for is under assault. Everything that was absolutely foundational in the establishment of our nation—perhaps not a *Christian* nation as some would define, but a nation significantly framed and shaped by Judeo-Christian principles—is being shaken.

Silent No More

The church cannot remain silent as the godless force of progressive liberalism transforms our communities, and our nation. Elton Trueblood, a Harvard chaplain turned theologian, was asked, "What do you see for the church of Jesus Christ by the year 2000?"

His answer was startling: "By the year 2000, the church will be a conscious minority surrounded by an arrogant, militant paganism."[8]

This question was asked in the early 1970s and Trueblood was not far off in his prediction. The signs were all present in 2000, and so much more so now in 2016. Christians are discovering that, like it or not, they are being pushed into the middle of controversies they would rather avoid. Welcome to the Coliseum. This may actually be a good thing.

Welcome to the Coliseum

It is time that American Christians understood why the Founding Fathers set up the system as they did. We need to understand how religious freedom is indispensable to the freedoms all enjoy, and we need to understand how the erosion of religion results in the collapse of all freedoms.

Persecution has its benefits. The Body of Christ needs something to produce the awakening that is needed. The loss of freedom will first agitate but then catalyze the 30 percent of the American population who self-describe as "Christian." This expression of persecution will mobilize the latent potential of the body of Christ into an actualized force to advance the kingdom.

We will discover what metal we are made of in the crucible. Let us pray it doesn't take an economic meltdown, before we will organize and deploy our influence both locally and nationally.

The Fourth Crucible

I am convinced the fourth crucible is upon us and the deception is an old design, sourced in Marxist/Lenin doctrine: lie, divide and conquer. That same spiritual and ideological battle has resumed today in hyper drive and goes deeper than the labels we now have of "liberal," "conservative," "democrat," or "republican."

The ideologies in tension are those of radical progressives seeking to:

- Implement Socialist Marxist solutions to economic issues.

- Do away with the checks and balances between the branches of governments by centralizing power through executive order.

- Lay waste to American fundamental liberties prescribed by our Founding Fathers. With a liberal majority, Supreme Court rulings will further undo the fundamental liberties that are already being eroded.

- Regulate, or even remove, the right to religious freedom and free speech. Soon any free speech perceived as intolerant "hate speech" from critical right wing media will be shut down. Can you imagine, the internet and radio being regulated? Pulpits needing to supply transcripts of messages that will be reviewed for possible violations.

- Remove the right for to bear arms, this will most likely be justified as a measure to address civil unrest.

The tension between world powers is already evident, but the devil is not the one in control. The writer of Hebrews tells us, "*When God spoke from Mount Sinai his voice shook the earth, but now he makes another promised, 'Once again I will shake not only the earth but the heavens also'*" (Hebrews 12:26).

ONCE AGAIN GOD IS SHAKING NOT ONLY THE EARTH, BUT THE HEAVENS ALSO

We are already standing on the tipping point, right in the middle of the perfect storm. We are one crisis away, that has a large enough impact on the American economy, before The Great American Reset is ushered in. When that time comes, because it's inevitable, the governing philosophy that will shape your new American reality—your status quo—will be determined by who gets elected in 2016.

Let's seize the opportunity that's standing before us and truly make this moment our **finest hour**!

Endnotes

1. Retrieved from http://www.abrahamlincolnonline. org/lincoln/speeches/lyceum.htm.

2. Retrieved from http://www.huffingtonpost.com/mayhill-fowler/obama-no-surprise-that-ha_b_96188.html.

3. Retrieved from http://www.hughhewitt.com/supreme-court-stupid/.

4. Retrieved from http://www.winstonchurchill.org/resources/ speeches/1940-the-finest-hour/122-their-finest-hour.

5. Retrieved from http://www.the-highway.com/articleOct01.html.

6. Retrieved from https://books.google.com/books?id=KTiTxlrY9AC& pg=PA119&lpg=PA119&dq=individuals+ground+their+views+of+the+ world+within+some+conception+of+moral&source=bl&ots=JsgjjiguH 0&sig=v8wOzM19WM9R7VAI_nENlArUnck&hl=en&sa=X&ved= 0ahUKEwj_6tjqk6fPAhXh7IMKHR6lBnMQ6AEIHjAA#v=onepa ge&q=individuals%20ground%20their%20views%20of%20the%20 world%20within%20some%20conception%20of%20moral&f=false.

7. Retrieved from https://www.rutherford.org/publications_resources/oldspeak/ christians_under_the_scripture_a_lecture_by_dr_francis_schaeffer_part_2.

8. Retrieved from http://www.ravenhill.org/weeping1.htm.

CHAPTER 10

THE UNFINISHED ASSIGNMENT

I had just finished recording a podcast. After I hung up the phone, I went to look at an article I had coming out in a magazine about Trump/ Pence. At first I was taken back by the title given to my article: "Why I believe Trump is the Prophesied President." Oh boy. I wondered, Will *people think I am actually prophesying that Trump will be president? After all, I've been saying that this guy should be president, right?* That's why I wrote this book. Trump has the Isaiah 45 Cyrus anointing. I believe there is unprecedented warfare over this election because so much is at stake. I also believe that Christians can be the decisive vote if they push past media mind control and hear what people like me are saying, or prophesying, depending on how they read the title of the article.

I knew that that once the magazine article was out, people would think I was prophesying a Trump win no matter what I said. So be it. Sometimes my life reminds me of a baseball story. There was an umpire named Beans Reardon. He made a mistake. As the dynamic center fielder named Richie Ashburn slid into second base the guy covering second, Billy Cox, went to tag him. Beans yelled "SAFE!" while simultaneously throwing his arm in the "You're OUT!" gesture.

Ashburn looked up and said, "what the hell does that mean?" Beans Reardon replied, "Richie you know he's safe. Billy you know he's safe. But 30,000 fans are looking at my arm. Richie, you're out." Sometimes there is just nothing you can do to control what people think you mean or don't mean by the things you say.

For the last three years, Acts 27 has been constantly coming to mind. I can't escape it. I believe this powerful chapter in the history of Paul speaks to several themes we will see played out in the days and years to come. It describes how God can overrule the folly of man and not only deliver us from the storms of life, but bring us into unexpected new territory that expands the kingdom.

Study this chapter and you will see how a figure started out with little influence over people but ended up redirecting events and shaping the future. It's a story that displays the power of an unfinished apostolic assignment. When you read it, think of the United States.

A Storm, a Ship, and a Divine Reversal

Acts 27 tells the story of the Apostle Paul who, while under Roman arrest, received a word from the Lord that he was to stand trial before Caesar in Rome. He was placed under Roman custody and boarded a ship to Rome. But as they sailed, Paul was divinely warned that there was danger ahead. The Bible doesn't say how he was warned, just that he knew what the future held if they kept sailing. He brought this warning to the those in charge saying, *"Men, I perceive that this voyage will end with disaster and much loss, not only of cargo and ship, but also our own lives"* (Acts 27:10).

Paul urged them to stay put in the harbor until the season passed, but it was a lousy harbor to spend the winter in. They had their mind set on Phoenix, a city with a lot more options for enjoying a port in the winter. They put it all to a vote and the majority overruled Paul. The centurion, ship's captain and owner decided to ignore the religious fanatic and the merry crew sailed on.

Once at sea, the ship was seized by a storm so vicious that they lost control of the vessel. In desperation, the crew began throwing cargo overboard and, soon after, the ship's tackle. As seasoned sailors gave up hope of survival, Paul kept pressing into a realm of apostolic intercession that broke into divine deliverance. Late in the night an angel appeared and told him, *"Do not be afraid, Paul. You must be brought before Caesar; and indeed, God has granted you all those who are sailing with you."* (Acts 27:24). The original word he received about going to Rome was still in force. In fact, the tables were about to turn entirely.

Paul was watching a divine reversal. He was no longer sailing with them—they were sailing with him! Paul, the prisoner, was delivered from death and all those that sailed with him were now prisoners on board God's obedience school. The ship soon ran aground near an island and was broken apart by the violence of the waves. All on board swam to shore, alive, just as the angel promised. The island was called Malta. From the moment he arrived, Paul owned that island. Beginning with a poisonous viper bite that didn't kill him, Paul was the epicenter of a signs and wonders move that impacted all the natives on Malta. They loved his ministry. The name "Malta" is translated as "honey or sweet spot" in many Greek texts. While the Romans waited for a new ship to come, the apostle took over the island. You can just imagine all 270 of the sailors waiting to see Paul give a thumbs up signal before boarding the ship for the voyage to Rome.

I think about this chapter and its application to America's unraveling. This text tells us we can shape the future if we are traveling in fulfillment of God's prophetic purpose.

While praying over this scripture, a few thoughts come to mind. We are all on board a ship.

- You may be the lowest ranking person on the ship, but if you're the only believer, you are the highest ranking spiritual authority.

- Just because you have perception doesn't mean the majority won't make a bad decision.

- Your greatest argument against death is an unfinished assignment.

One could observe this account as an illustration, showing the unique interaction between three influential spheres of our day: church, government and economics. Think of Paul as the church on board the ship of State. Paul is on board but not in charge. The Centurion represents the government. The Captain and owner of the ship could represent business and economics. These three spheres are not enemies, they simply are not working together. The truth is, America is presently being navigated by powerful interests and ideologies that are moving contrary to the nation's prophetic assignment. The ship is heading into an unnecessary storm; the church, just like the Apostle Paul, is being led into a storm scenario.

In the Acts 27 account, God wasn't sending a storm. He was trying to help them avoid it! In the end, what saved all their lives was the fact that Paul was on board their ship. His commitment to his unfinished assignment pulled them through a disaster. Even though our country would appear to be heading toward stormy conditions, the praying church is still "on board" the ship—and we along with our nation have an unfinished assignment. In Paul's account he went from being ignored and overruled to being the key man on the ship to help them survive. What if the church is called to do something like this? What if the island of Malta is the unexplored territory of the Gospel breaking out in communities in ways never seen before? What if the ship is dismantled and we have to wait until the new ship is built or arrives? How might that apply to our situation? Think of different scenarios.

The Unfinished Assignment of America

The great revivalist Charles Finney said, "make your calling your constant argument with God for all that you have need of in its accomplishment." Finney was a lawyer who was powerfully converted and became an evangelist. By saying to make your calling your "argument," he meant make your assignment the basis of your petition. Our "case" or argument in the storm cannot be that America deserves to be delivered. Nor should we plead that God should deliver America because He loves America. God loves

> MAKE YOUR CALLING YOUR CONSTANT ARGUMENT WITH GOD FOR ALL THAT YOU HAVE IN NEED OF ITS ACCOMPLISHMENT

other nations in crisis too. He loves Syria, Iraq, Ukraine, Greece and Venezuela just as much as He loves us.

Perhaps we should be asking: "What is America's unfinished assignment in the world? What have we been so uniquely blessed to do that we have not done?" America is here to be a blessing to the nations of the earth. We are here to not only spread the Gospel but to provide stability to the world as the Gospel does its work in other nations. Paul was spared because he had a divine appointment in Rome. It was not his time to die. Likewise, America is too young to die.

The mission of America is more than preaching salvation. The fact that there are underground churches all over the world is a testament to the Gospel being preached faithfully for generations. In addition, the Gospel is accessible on satellite, internet, radio and print media like never before. America has played a role in this, supporting work around the world. But is our assignment finished? I say no. The redemptive gifts of this nation include "innovation" and "leadership." The mission movement has been stagnant for years because we missed the window to the next phase of the Great Commission. The call to "go into all the world" is no longer simply geographic. We must go into all the "systems" of this world—the seven mountains or seven mind molders of culture. We must become a "7m™" movement. We have to look at Daniel in Babylon and see how this works. Daniel had three friends who shared a similar calling. They met as a small group in a house in Babylon. When necessary they prayed, and when they did Daniel operated in supernatural gifts. If Daniel could do this in the Old Testament what should we be able to do under the New Covenant based on better promises than Daniel had?

When you go into the "systems" of this world, you invade strongholds. It's not wise or necessary to do this by yourself. Daniel had three companions. It requires a different level of kingdom authority to deal with the gates of hell. Jesus said, *"I will build My church and the gates of Hell will not prevail against it."* (Matthew 16:18). The word for "church" in the New Testament is the word *ecclesia*. The world of Jesus' day knew this word as it was used throughout the Roman empire to refer to the method of civil governing by political bodies. The word was used as far back as the time of Alexander the Great to describe the governing bodies of Greek city states. The *ecclesia* is a governing word describing a governing body of believers called out as citizens of the kingdom to take their seats at the gates! What gates? The gates of influence that shape the cities and nations of the earth. Is that how you think of church? By moving in small groups to advance as believers we are exploring a new mission movement, and it is way overdue. This new entity is called a "micro-church." We need them in every 7m sphere where the gates of influence are dominated by "tares" and not "wheat." We need to look for the Cyruses among them. We need to be modern day Esthers, Josephs, Daniels and Nehemiahs. By advancing up your mountain with a small group that knows how to pray, your 7m micro-church becomes a "force multiplier." You become the front line of a new mission movement!

Suffice it to say, America plays a huge role in the world as a force for freedom and the preaching of the Gospel. So much so that Satan considers taking this nation down to be his number one priority. With us removed, hell can advance against the church globally. Weaker democracies will falter. A new era of "strongman"

> AMERICA PLAYS A HUGE ROLE IN THE WORLD AS A FORCE FOR FREEDOM AND THE PREACHING OF THE GOSPEL

populism will start emerging. The United States has held the door of democracy open. Satan intends to shut it. By now I hope you can see that this is far beyond a battle of politics. It's not a matter of party versus party, Republican against Democrat. We are up against a malevolent and demonic agenda aimed to destroy the global force for kingdom expansion that is America. Our failure to take seriously the discipling of nations is the failure of the modern church. The coming storm will change that. Innovation and leadership is about to emerge in a global movement of believers.

The Counter-Assignment Against America

Satan, well aware of America's unique assignment to globally advance the discipleship of nations, recognizes the influence of what we export. At present, we are experiencing a great unraveling because somebody else discipled the nation. Let's own it. There are reasons behind our demise:

- Christians are not taught the Gospel of the kingdom. To a great extent, ministers and ministries do not train people to expand the kingdom through their careers and callings in life.

- We do not work together or mobilize believers in their spheres to advance the Gospel of the kingdom in our communities.

- The World system has evangelized the church with its values and influence. We seek the same goals, namely affluence and significance. The difference between us and progressives is that Christians are reluctant to offend the political correctness of Babylon.

- Believers are taught escapist theology. This comes through the guise of seeking ever-deeper spiritual experiences, or the erroneous belief that things will change in nations if we just become more spiritual ourselves. By not focusing on going into all the world's systems we bottle up the antidote! The corruption that rules the 7 mountains of nations does not stay still, it spreads and counteracts the transformational power of the Gospel. By isolating ourselves from the systems of justice, law, literature, art, etc. we fail to be the healing force to change the nations and the nations get worse. Eventually, this will deteriorate into a status where the church itself comes under siege.

The ultimate problem is the way the church defines itself. The church is Christ's *ecclesia*—His government on the earth. The Left advanced and took over spheres of influence that Christian morality once held. For a long time there was a balance. We have lost the common moral ground from which differences can be resolved.

I'm doing my best to be a voice in this book pointing toward Donald Trump and saying, like the Apostle Paul did in Acts 27:10— *"Sirs, this is what I perceive."* What happens electorally in America (in a matter of days) will affect the world. The tension between world powers is already evident. Russia is reasserting itself in the Middle East. Iran is being resuscitated by American policy and cash. China is flexing its muscles and expanding its military reach in the China sea, all while North Korea completes its fifth nuclear demonstration. We're no longer living in a unipolar world where America can single-handedly dictate terms to everybody else. Something major is shifting. **How will you respond?**

What is America's Role in the World?

Since the fall of the Soviet Union, the United States has without question been the world's dominant economic and military force. It is a super power without equal. An argument can be made that the last time this occurred in world history was the Roman Empire. At the height of Rome's power, its military was used to maintain revenue streams to Rome through domination, slavery, and cultural coercion.

The United States uses its power to maintain world stability so that each component part of the world can function as it sees fit for its own purposes and cultural values. The U.S. is the first super power not to use its military or economic might to oppress its competitors or non-citizens.

I asked a friend, Mark Nuttle, who has served various presidents to share his perspective on America's role in the world. In his personal report (available at www.marcnuttle.com) here is what he wrote:

Geopolitical

The United States military is the only worldwide force that keeps the world from breaking apart at the seams. If the U.S. shrunk in its military commitment and withdrew to its borders, within weeks, if not days, China would threaten Taiwan, Pakistan and India would continue border skirmishes that would escalate, Columbia and Venezuela would have internal difficulties maintaining treaties with their neighbors, Russia would be unchecked in bullying its former Soviet neighbors, the Middle East would explode, and non-state states like ISIS, Al Qaida and war lords worldwide would move about with abandon. Literally, the world would become regional danger zones with pirates operating in between regions.

For commerce to continue worldwide, sea lanes must remain open, particularly narrow lanes like the Straits of Hormuz. It may be possible to coordinate the British Navy with other local authorities, but such an organization does not exist and there are not enough navies worldwide to coordinate to keep the oceans safe. Only the United States has the capacity to perform this service.

Economics

The United States consumes 50% of all goods and services in the world. If our markets were to decline, the world would go into depression. Further, we are the only true free enterprise system in the world. We are less regulated and less restricted than most countries. The reason that Japan is able to pay its government bills with very little growth internally is because Toyota can come to the U.S., manufacture cars, sell them worldwide, and pay some taxes back to Japan. Germany, Great Britain, France and Italy all sell high-end goods in the United States, creating jobs and revenue for their economies.

Finances

The United States is the world's largest banking system. Other countries have large banks, but the size and diversity of the U.S. banking system is unparalleled. The size, depth and diversity of the U.S. banking system is necessary to finance consumer loans worldwide.

The most important value that the United States currently provides for the world is its currency. In my opinion, the dollar is not the world's secondary currency; it is its primary currency. International commodities critical to the world's commerce are traded in dollars. There are 184 countries, including observer countries, that are members of the World Trade Organization. Many of the smaller countries could not operate their small economies without a true world currency—like the dollar—in which they can maneuver to produce their goods and services. Without the dollar, the world would have to operate on regional currencies, possibly the Euro and some new emerging currency designed by China, Russia or their partners. Any transition to regional currencies would take years to assimilate all the world's goods and services into a normal flow of exchange rates. The smaller economies could not weather the transition and would most likely collapse. This is why it is so important that the United States manage its currency prudently, not just for itself, but for the world.

What is America's Future?

As we move into October, 2016, let's pray that this Hebrew calendar year 5777 becomes a true Jubilee year when God intervenes and uses the unraveling and crucible to forge something new and cancel the debt we cannot cancel on our own without Him.

I am convinced that God is not finished with America. Malta was a place of supernatural visitation. It was as if God said, "Because you tried to destroy my servant, I am going to give him all those that sail with him and throw an entire island in for good measure!"

GOD IS NOT FINISHED WITH AMERICA

I believe America is supposed to be strong because we are needed to bring stability to the world so that the Gospel of the kingdom can advance and nations can actually be brought to the kingdom. This was the vision Jesus gave his disciples. To make disciples of nations, we must teach them not to do as we have done. We must rise up and strengthen those things that yet remain in America and begin to push back the darkness.

As this awareness hits the slumbering saints, it will rock them into mobilization at a level not yet seen in our lifetime.

I believe America will enter this season of advancing the kingdom regardless of what party is in power, but I believe God would spare us unnecessary trauma and loss by heeding what the Lord says.

This book, *God's Chaos Candidate* was released in October 2016 (one month from the general election) during the Feast of Trumpets.

This opens the Hebrew year 5777, a Jubilee year. This Jubilee occurs every 70 years. According to Hebrew teaching, this is a time when God intervenes and cancels out debt. It is a time of new beginnings. If Trump is elected, he will be 70 years old when he enters office. Is it too much to believe that God is having his way in the whirlwind and providing a man who is gifted to navigate through the chaos of the next season until we arrive safely on the other side of the Fourth Crucible.

The next season in America will be a time of both grace and spiritual warfare in the clashing of spiritual swords, ideas and spokesman. I believe God will use the pressure of circumstance to forge something new for the United States. Remember Malta! God is not finished with America and America needs you to press into your unfinished assignment. The church needs a kingdom version of Thunder Road to put an end to the disjointed and competing elements of our movement.

What would this look like? In the future we will study William Wilberforce and see the nonviolent model that attacked racism, ended slavery, and restored Christian values to what had become a decadent slave trading nation. We need to rise up AS ONE and participate in the unfolding of God's strategy. Expect God's trumpets to awaken the slumbering saints and rock them into mobilization at a level not yet seen in our lifetime. As One!

So far what I've predicted has come true. There's not much time left for us to act. Visit **www.godschaoscandidate.com/movement** and join the movement today!

SNAPSHOT OF THE 2016 REPUBLICAN PARTY PLATFORM

Following is a brief summary of the positions taken by the Republican Party to form their 2016 party platform:[1]

Marriage

The American family is the foundation of civil society and the cornerstone is marriage, the union of one man and one woman ... we do not accept the Supreme Court's redefinition of marriage and we urge its reversal, whether through judicial reconsideration or a constitutional amendment returning control over marriage to the States.

The Supreme Court and Marriage

We condemn the Supreme Court's ruling in *United States v. Windsor*, which wrongfully removed the ability of Congress to define marriage policy in federal law. We also condemn the Supreme Court's ruling in *Obergefell v. Hodges*, which in the words of the late Justice Antonin Scalia was a "judicial Putsch"—"full of silly extravagances"—that "reduced the disciplined legal reasoning of John Marshall and Joseph Story to the mythical aphorisms of a fortune cookie." In *Obergefell*, five unelected lawyers robbed 320 million Americans of their legitimate constitutional authority to define marriage as the union of one man and one woman. The Court twisted the meaning of the Fourteenth Amendment beyond recognition. To echo Scalia, we dissent. We therefore support the appointment of justices and judges who respect the constitutional limits on their power and respect the authority of the states to decide such fundamental social questions.

Protecting Human Life

The Constitution's guarantee that no one can "be deprived of life, liberty or property" deliberately echoes the Declaration of Independence's proclamation that "all" are "endowed by their Creator" with the inalienable right to life. Accordingly, we assert the sanctity of human life and affirm that the unborn child has a fundamental right to life which cannot be infringed. We support a human life amendment to the Constitution and legislation to make clear that the Fourteenth Amendment's protections apply to children before birth. We oppose the use of public funds to perform or promote abortion or to fund organizations, like Planned Parenthood.

Education—Title IX

We emphatically support the original, authentic meaning of Title IX of the Education Amendments of 1972. It affirmed that "no person in the United States shall, on the basis of sex, be excluded from participation in, be denied the benefits of, or be subjected to discrimination under any education program or activity receiving Federal financial assistance." That language opened up for girls and women a world of opportunities that had too often been denied to them. That same provision of law is now being used by bureaucrats—and by the current president of the United States—to impose a social and cultural revolution upon the American people by wrongly redefining sex discrimination to include sexual orientation, or other categories. The agenda has nothing to do with individual rights; it has everything to do with power. They are —determined to reshape our schools or entire society—to fit the mold of an ideology alien to America's history and traditions. Their edict to the States concerning restrooms, locker rooms and other facilities is at once illegal, dangerous, and ignores privacy issues. We salute the several states which have filed suit against it.

Our National Defense

We believe that our nation is most secure when the president and the administration prioritize readiness, recruitment, and retention, rather than using the military to advance a social or political agendas. Military readiness must not be sacrificed on the altar of politically correct social agendas, which this administration has done.

Safe Neighborhoods

The next president must restore the public's trust in law enforcement and civil order, by first adhering to the rule of law himself. Additionally, the next president must cease the sowing the seeds of division and distrust between the police and the people they have sworn to serve and protect. The Republican Party, a party of law and order, must make clear in words and actions that every human life matters.

Economic Growth

Republicans consider the establishment of a pro-growth tax code a moral imperative.

We condemn attempts by activist judges at any level of government to seize the power of the purse from the people's elected representatives by ordering higher taxes.

Republican budgets will prioritize thrift over extravagance and put taxpayers first. We support the following test: Is a particular expenditure within the constitutional scope of the federal government? If not, stop it.

Health Care

Any honest agenda for improving health care must start with repeal of the dishonestly named Affordable Care Act of 2010: Obamacare. It weighs like the dead hand of the past upon American medicine.

Endnotes

1. This summary of the 2016 Republican Party Platform is adapted from Breitbart. Retrieved from: http://www.breitbart.com/2016-presidential-race/2016/07/18/republicans-adopt-conservative-platform-modern-history/.

JOIN THE MOVEMENT!

The future of this nation is in the hands of the church—the people of God. That's you!

Make no mistake, God still has an unfinished assignment for America. It's time to recognize the integral role you play in the unfolding of God's prophetic purposes:

- Your individual callings have a pivotal role in God's agenda being accomplished on Earth as it is in Heaven.

- Your prayers have strategic intercessory impact in the unseen realm and impact the course of world history.

- Your voice has a direct say in the outcome of elections, policies, and the direction of nation.

WWW.GODSCHAOSCANDIDATE.COM/MOVEMENT

The Great Commission has not changed since Jesus left the earth. His vision was and is to see nations discipled.

Join me and thousands of others as we shape the course of nations one voice at a time.